PUBLIC SPEAKING IN

PUBLIC SPEAKING IN BUSINESS

How to make a success of meetings, speeches, conferences and all business presentations

Stuart Turner

McGRAW-HILL BOOK COMPANY

London · New York · San Francisco · Auckland · Bogotá
Caracas · Hamburg · Lisbon · Madrid · Mexico · Milan
Montreal · New Delhi · Panama · Paris · San Juan · São
Paulo · Singapore · Sydney · Tokyo · Toronto

Published by
McGRAW-HILL Book Company Europe
Shoppenhangers Road, Maidenhead, Berkshire, SL6 2QL, England
Telephone 0628 23432
Fax 0628 770224

British Library Cataloguing in Publication Data

Turner, Stuart
 Public speaking in business.
 I. Title
 808.51

ISBN 0-07-707559-5

Library of Congress Cataloging-in-Publication Data

Turner, Stuart
  Public speaking in business : how to make a success of
 meetings, speeches, conferences and all business
 presentations / Stuart Turner.
   p. cm.
  Includes index.
  ISBN 0-07-707559-5 (pbk.)
  1. Business presentations. 2. Public speaking. I. Title.
 HF5718.22.T87   1991
 658.4′52—dc20   91-22740

Copyright © 1991 McGraw-Hill International (UK) Limited.
All rights reserved. No part of this publication may be
reproduced, stored in a retrieval system, or transmitted, in any
form or by any means, electronic, mechanical, photocopying,
recording, or otherwise, without the prior permission of
McGraw-Hill International (UK) Limited.

Designed and typeset by Plexus Design Consultants, Aldershot
Printed and bound in Great Britain by Dotesios Limited, Trowbridge

For Annie Hallam and Jane French at The Right Address.
They know why.

Contents

Introduction

1	Objectives	1
2	Who do you think you are talking to?	7
3	What have you got to say for yourself?	19
4	Talks, lectures and special occasions	35
5	Have you heard the one about...?	49
6	Remembering the words	57
7	Visual aids	67
8	Rehearsals	87
9	Getting on with your nerves	97
10	Countdown	105
11	Being heard	117
12	Stand and deliver	123
13	Taking the chair	137
14	Interview techniques	149
15	Behind the scenes	163
16	Venues	179
17	Paperwork	193
18	Debriefing	199

Index 205

INTRODUCTION

Despite the relentless march of technology, it is unlikely that the VDU will ever totally replace the human voice as a means of communication. The ability to speak well in public will remain important. A good speaker can, among other things, communicate ideas and get them accepted, motivate staff, influence opinions, inform customers and promote a new product or cause (not least a personal career perhaps).

Possibly because of nerves, many business people shy away from opportunities to speak, or take refuge in marching to the podium and reading every word from a binder or cueing system. With a little thought and effort it is possible to do much better than that; I hope this book will help in the process.

Stuart Turner

1
OBJECTIVES

Seminars, symposiums, workshops, conferences, meetings...the list of functions at which business people may be speaking is endless. But whatever the function, the first thing to do is vow never to blabber away just for the sake of it; you must have a clearly defined purpose, you must have clear, businesslike objectives. Even if you have relatively little control over where and when you are speaking because you are presenting to customers on their own premises and may be at their beck and call, you should still plan your approach carefully to maximize your chances of success. If you are speaking at a meeting initiated by you or your company, ask yourself if you are really just calling people together because it has become an annual ritual. Not a strong enough reason. Getting people together costs money — quite a lot of it if you include salaries, accommodation, travel and entertaining (not to mention lost sales while your representatives are quaffing your coffee) — so do consider carefully if all the effort and expense will be justified. However, when evaluating whether to call, say, a field-force together for a meeting, don't ignore the subjective but none the less valuable benefit that may accrue simply from people gathering together. Folks like to feel part of a group and staff will function better if camaraderie builds up; quite often the exchange of views over a drink will be more productive than a speaker's careful presentation.

At many functions the speeches and presentations seem designed just to fill in the time and are more for sitting through than listening to — try to give your words more meaning.

It is a good discipline to write down your objectives in making a speech or presentation. And don't be too bland in doing so; it is too easy to settle for an important sounding but fairly meaningless objective, just as many company visions and mission statements come close to waffling on about motherhood and kindness to animals. Be more specific.

Where relevant, try to *quantify* what you are hoping to achieve; for instance, if you are telling employees about the benefits of being paid by cheque, write down what percentage you hope will eventually switch from cash. If you are launching a new product, decide if your main objective is to inform people about it or to motivate them to go out and break sales records with it; the approaches could be different.

Don't have too many objectives in mind otherwise you will simply confuse people and may fail to meet fully any objective. Jotting down your aims will help you to establish whether you are trying to inform, sell, motivate or entertain with your words; you should usually try to entertain irrespective of your other aims, if you are to stop your audience mentally tuning out or even going to sleep. Launching a new product? Well, if you don't make a song and dance about it, rest assured that no one else will; if you don't shout about it to motivate your salesforce, they may think you are not very excited by it and conclude that it can't be very good or worthwhile.

YOUR MESSAGE

Whatever the occasion, as well as considering your objectives, be clear what messages you are trying to get across and don't have too many or you will just confuse your audience. And do recognize that it may be difficult to change people's minds during a peroration. You may persuade them that a new product has merit, but if retailers are convinced that your discount structure is out of line with your competitor's then only drastic action and/or a very persuasive presentation is likely to convince them otherwise. Accept too that it may be difficult to shift a well-entrenched falsehood. If your company has had grossly unfair coverage in the press you will have to work very hard to overcome the conclusion 'Yes, but there's no smoke...'. More positively, a speech can be used to signal a negotiating position (a ploy politicians regularly use) while if a point you make is picked up and used elsewhere you may have an influence on opinion.

If nothing else, if you perform well when speaking to general audiences you may have an influence on the opinion they have of business people. Executives may be shown in surveys to be more trusted than politicians or journalists, but they fall a long way behind even soap opera stars in audience appeal, 'boring' being the word many people would perhaps use to describe business folk. Try to show them otherwise.

To help the process the last few chapters of this book look at things from the event organizer's point of view, because to be a really successful speaker you need to have a 'feel' for an occasion and what is going on around you. The more you understand what makes a successful function, the more effective you will be as a speaker.

If you are speaking at a conference and are also involved in the organization, decide at an early stage what information flow you want. Is it to be one-way, with a series of presentations to an audience? Well, if so, only the words stand between them and slumber. However, while an element of participation is highly desirable, be a shade wary of inviting comment during a major presentation to launch a new product; wild euphoria may be deflated if just one grumpy individual asks an awkward question or poses a counter-view to what was put across.

If those present are expected to 'cascade' information downwards to subordinates, then this should be made clear at the start (it will make them pay attention) and supporting material — printed extracts, slides or whatever — should be made available to help the communication process. If you don't provide a basic backbone of such material then delegates will be forced to pass on their own interpretation of what was said. If in turn their presentations are further cascaded by others down the company tree, then messages can become fairly distorted before they reach the troops who, in reality, probably have most need of a totally accurate brief. So...provide support material for any cascade exercise.

Incidentally, whatever your aims and objectives, take care not to get out of your depth when speaking. Because of the power of the media we tend to deify too easily and those who may be skilled or famous in one area, such as a sport, are solemnly asked for their views on more worldly matters such as politics; worse, they are sometimes unwise enough to pontificate and make fools of themselves in the process. Business people should not fall into the same trap. Stick to what you know because knowledge of a subject, however badly presented, is better than well-delivered waffle.

To summarize the chapter: be quite clear what your objectives are in making a speech or giving a presentation, and consider what messages you want to put across. In other words, be as businesslike about the process as you would be (I hope) about any other aspect of your business life.

In case you need a quick refresher course at any time, checklists are included at the end of each chapter highlighting the key points. The first is overleaf.

Checklist 1

- [ ] Why are you holding the meeting?

- [ ] Is it *really* necessary?

- [ ] Write down your objectives. Quantify when possible.

- [ ] What messages do you hope to put across? (Avoid too many.)

- [ ] Is information to flow two ways?

- [ ] Will support material be needed if information is to be cascaded downwards?

2
WHO DO YOU THINK YOU ARE TALKING TO?

Audiences are what speeches and presentations are all about — or should be. The message that gets across in a speech is not what you *think* you have said but what your audience actually *understands* you to have said, so if you take away no other message from this book, take this: *Keep thinking of your audience.* And be quite clear who your real audience is, by the way. A politician may deliver a weighty address containing controversial comments to a handful of people in a small village hall — his *real* audience will be the general public, which he hopes to reach via press releases of his words and, he will hope, radio and TV coverage. In such a case a small audience is simply being used as a convenient launching pad to reach a wider group. Such an approach will be carefully planned but remember that, if the media are present when you speak, a few hard-hitting words — perhaps added at the last minute to liven up a dull gathering — may be picked up and delivered to a far wider audience than you ever intended or desired. If you ever speak with a live TV camera trained on you then do remember the effect your words may have on that (much) wider audience. At a smaller, less formal level several motor industry executives have been alarmed to find an apparently innocent remark about gloomy sales prospects at an overseas motor show blown up into 'Job losses likely' stories back home.

With these warnings in mind, let us consider your 'live' audience. Find out as much as possible about them before speaking, because a proper analysis will guide you on how to pitch things. Is the audience attending voluntarily or have people been dragooned into coming? Are they attending out of a sense of duty? Are they members of a trade association and, if so, have you joined or at least kept in touch with the same one? What mood is the audience likely to be in? A reader can turn a page if bored or irritated by the words but your audience will be stuck with you and you need folks ready to listen if a meeting is to be a success. This is going to sound awfully patronizing but... how intelligent is the audience likely to be? If in doubt, flatter them by overestimating their intelligence — better probably to leave dimmer delegates a shade puzzled because they didn't follow your more erudite remarks than to offend the brighter people by presenting entirely in a 'cat sat on the mat' mode. Incidentally, if you feel that you are cleverer than the audience, don't for heaven's sake make it obvious that you have this opinion.

How 'international' are they? Not necessarily in their nationalities but in their exposure to the great wide world, to other cultures. It could affect the level at which you pitch things.

APPROACH

You could need a different approach for an audience of carpet sales staff than you would use for university professors. It's obvious which would be the quickest audience, of course — the sales people because they would be more in tune with everyday life than the professors; it might slow your rhythm to have to keep breaking off with the latter to explain who Joan Collins is. Above all, what will the audience be expecting from you? Try not to disappoint them. What links do you personally have with the audience? Will they regard you as 'for' or 'against' them, as friend or foe? Will they be friendly towards you or sit there bristling with hostility and virtually challenging you to break through to them?

If you will be speaking to customers, try to analyse their attitudes to you and your company. Do you have close links with them and do they love your product? Or do they use your product but would be equally happy to use someone else's at a similar price? Maybe they are even attending your presentation under some sufferance and are, if anything, unfriendly towards you. Again, this analysis could affect your approach to them.

Your invitation to speak may, of course, come from an outside source — perhaps a social group wanting you to speak about your profession. If so, consider who the organizers are and whether you are in sympathy with them and their aims. Is it an important audience for you or your message? Conversely and perhaps cynically, is it an *unimportant* audience? In which case you may decide not to waste your time or to use the occasion mainly to build up experience as a speaker.

Why have *you* been asked? Don't preen too readily if you are approached to speak — it may be that the organization simply has to find a speaker every month and has turned to you in some desperation. Worse, they may actually be hostile and have invited you with a view to giving you a roasting, perhaps with the media present. Keep in mind that while business people may be well regarded, nay even loved, in their own cloistered world, 'business', especially 'big business', is not universally worshipped. If you are the combative type you may well relish the chance to tackle a hostile group (more power to you) but at least know what you are letting yourself in for.

If, after the careful consideration suggested, you accept an invitation to speak, you need to know the day and date of the function; always ask for both to avoid any misunderstanding. Having established 'who' and 'when', you next need to know 'where'. Do get clear directions for finding a venue plus a phone number in case of any emergency. Most people are poor at giving directions and few will know road numbers, but persevere and, for instance, establish if there is a major landmark, such as a pub, near to the venue. A good organizer will advise you of complicated one-way systems while the more thoughtful ones may send you a map and then reserve parking space for you and have someone on the lookout when you arrive to make you feel welcome. But don't bank on it. If an overnight stay is involved, book in at the venue itself if possible to simplify your travel movements.

FEES

If you become a seasoned speaker and part of the speaking circuit (such fame) you may need to consider what fee to charge, if any. However amateur you are as a speaker, it is only reasonable that you should be reimbursed at least with your expenses, unless of course you are anxious for the opportunity to speak in order to put over a particular point or promote your company. You may be offered a few bottles of wine rather than a fee. Some organizations present speakers with mementoes, perhaps paintings of themselves. It can become an embarrassing area with vague phrases used like 'what arrangements do you have in mind?' instead of a more direct 'what fee do you charge?' Somewhat incredibly there are even organizations so full of their own importance that they give the impression it is such an honour to address them that speakers should pay rather than be paid. Anyway, if you are in business you will not be surprised to learn that market forces operate and speakers' fees vary according to their quality and of course their 'name'. Incidentally, if you are reluctant to accept a fee (and you shouldn't be because it only depresses the market for the rest of us) then consider taking a donation for your favourite charity instead.

Establish whether food will be served at the function so that you can plan your day accordingly; if you have a heavy lunch and then find you are faced with a five-course dinner before performing, you may be too bloated to speak well. I'm not suggesting that you need to jog regularly if you are a speaker, but it is fairly obvious you will be more at ease if your clothes aren't cutting you in half. And talking of clothes, what dress is to be worn? If it says 'dress optional' for a dinner, ask how many (if any) will be in evening dress and dress accordingly.

Find out what time the function will actually get under way — establish a realistic start time because organizers will often try to get you there far too early. Your promptness should depend on the occasion and whether you have to sort out slide equipment, etc. If you are one of a series of invited speakers at a conference, it makes sense to be there early enough to sit in on any previous speakers so that you can get a feel for the audience and modify your approach if necessary, perhaps to avoid duplication. For dinners, 7.30 for 8.00 usually means that people are called in around 8.10 although there are exceptions so it is worth checking in advance.

Ask the organizer how long you will be expected to speak. Keep in mind that most organizers are hopelessly optimistic about how long an audience will want to listen to you. Even the time of day may affect the length of your speech. For instance, knockabout humour or a long-winded approach will not be well received at breakfast meetings (which in my view should be banned anyway on humanitarian grounds). If you drone on at a lunch session you may hear, literally, the grating sound of chairs being moved as people leave, while if you speak too long after a dinner then an audience may get restless, particularly if they know dancing is to follow. When discussing such details with an organizer in the cold sober light of day, keep in mind the fact that whether alcohol will have been served before you speak may affect the response — sadly, you may not be able to predict this until the day: wine makes some audiences relaxed and receptive, others it may make belligerent and hostile.

An efficient organizer will confirm all the points in writing; make sure you have the business and home telephone numbers of someone you can call for information as the day draws near. This should be someone in tune with the organization because you may need advice as to whether a particular approach is likely to be well received.

Clearly, you may not need enormous detail if you are speaking to your own company, but don't become too casual if this is the case; for instance, if you are due to address a bunch of engineers and plan to joke about the head of manufacturing, it may be worth checking in advance whether he is going to be there, rather than be thrown by finding out just before you speak that he has been taken ill. Even worse would be to make some jokey reference while being the only one in the room *not* aware of his illness. The same care is needed to avoid making a gaffe over someone recently separated or known to be having an affair.

My stress on paying attention to detail may seem a shade nitpicking if you've just been asked to propose the loyal toast at a trade association dinner, but some of the above points may still apply. In contrast, there will be occasions when even more background information will help you to perform well (and I make no apology for considering a speech or presentation as something of a 'performance' — if you don't recognize that you will be on show and centre-stage while speaking, then you are unlikely to inspire anyone). For instance, who were the speakers at the last function and how well were they received? Knowing this will help to give you that all-important 'feel' for your audience and its expectations; if the organizer comments that 'so-and-so went on for hours about his sludge pumps', it should be taken as a hint not to dwell too long on your new product, at least not unless you can find a way of making it really enthralling. Who else is speaking and in what order? This may save you going into shock on the day if you suddenly find you are sandwiched between two household names. Incidentally, if you find you are just one of an interminable list of speakers, it may be time to back gracefully off the scene or at least vow to keep your address short. At formal business dinners, for instance, there will often be four speakers when three would be kinder to the audience, perhaps with the middle speaker responding to one toast before going on to propose another.

It helps to have an estimate of how many there will be in your audience and what age and sex they will be; the stronger 'pitched up' approach needed for a large gathering would be out of place with a smaller, more intimate group, while the dangers of preparing a ribald speech and then finding ladies in your audience are obvious. Not that I believe you should ever need to use ribald material, by the way; even if any women present are quite happy, men around them may be embarrassed, which will take the edge off things. Why take the risk?

Last but certainly not least in your audience analysis, you need to know what you are supposed to be speaking about. If an organizer invites you to 'Give us 20 minutes or so on whatever you feel like', try to get a more specific brief. If you don't, you may think he wanted you to speak about your company, and prepare accordingly, when in fact he wanted you to talk about the trophy you won for Morris dancing. I've heard a Euro MP speak for 25 minutes on a totally inappropriate theme to a trade association because he hadn't established which branch of the organization he was addressing and what they wanted from him. Establishing the subject matter may even cause you to pull out of a function if, say, an organizer keeps harping on about a subject that you simply don't want to talk about. Equally, being unable to get a clear brief from an organizer may be another reason for saying 'no' because it may indicate that you have been invited simply because, as mentioned earlier, the organization traditionally has a speaker without really knowing why.

Remember that no one can *force* you to speak and you certainly don't have to if you are just making up the numbers.

Clearly defining the subject matter for an address is important for business people who are invited to give 'keynote' speeches to conferences because the other presentations will, to some extent, be built around them. Incidentally, if you are speaking at a conference, I think you should resist requests to submit your speech several weeks in advance unless it is a very erudite and involved subject to a learned group. The world of business can change so fast that nothing with a long 'listen by date' is likely to enthrall an audience.

Finally, if you need a title for your address, make it as compelling as possible, particularly if it will be used to attract an audience. 'How I made a million' will be more compelling than 'The story of A. Company Ltd' although the words may remain the same. If a conference has a theme, as they often have, then relate your title to it and make one or two references to the theme during your pitch to make it more apposite.

CHECKLIST 2

☐ Which is your *real* audience? The live one or a wider public via the media?

☐ Why is the audience there? Willingly or under sufferance?

☐ What mood is the audience likely to be in?

☐ Are they colleagues, customers, suppliers, general public or...?

☐ If an outside invitation, are you in sympathy with the group's objectives?

☐ How intelligent, how worldly are they?

☐ How many?

☐ Age and sex?

☐ Day and date.

☐ Realistic start time.

☐ Venue and how to find it. Phone number.

☐ Fee and/or expenses?

☐ Catering arrangements.

☐ Dress.

☐ How long are you expected to speak? What about?

☐ Other speakers? Toasts?

☐ Name and phone number of a contact if you need more information.

☐ Title for your presentation.

3
WHAT HAVE YOU GOT TO SAY FOR YOURSELF?

The previous chapter stressed the importance of analysing audiences. Before you move on to prepare your words, it is worth spending a little time analysing yourself. I'm not suggesting you should rush for the psychologist's couch but do at least consider what sort of character you are or, more important, what sort of character your audience will perceive you to be. Obviously, if you are a sales director talking to a salesforce then there will be no identity crisis on either side. But if you, still as a sales director, are due to talk to an outside group, will they see you as an over-slick operator preying on innocent customers, or as someone who cares about giving good service or...? Will they see you as a dry person or a jovial one? Someone they can relate to? Or someone they will feel mild hostility towards (which will need to be overcome)?

I don't want to labour this point about self-analysis, but considering the sort of person your audience will perceive you to be will most emphatically help you when you come to prepare your words. Consider, for instance, how confused a theatre audience might become if a comedian in a check suit with a bright bow tie and a red nose started delivering droll material more suited to a laid-back individual in evening dress (or vice versa). Mind, whatever 'character' you are perceived to be by an audience, your reception will be greater and warmer if you make a lively, possibly humorous, presentation. An audience's delight may be greater if you — as an apparently dry old stick — are entertaining than if a known comic is, because the latter will of course be *expected* to amuse.

Having given some thought to how you will be perceived by your audience, you are ready to turn to a key part of making a speech or giving a presentation — preparing the words. 'Key' because it doesn't matter how smooth a speaker you are, or how elegant the venue, if you haven't got something worthwhile to say, you will not be a success. You may well develop your own methods for preparing your words but, as a guide, I suggest you consider going through the following process when you have received an invitation to speak:

1 Sit back and think generally about your subject matter.
2 Gather together any necessary supporting information.
3 Sort your thoughts and information into a sensible (i.e. logical) order.
4 Write your words.

If you are simply trying to sell a customer something in a face-to-face presentation, you may feel that all these stages are unnecessary, but they are not. In such circumstances you should in Stage 1 reflect on what the customer will be expecting from you; for instance, are there any problems with existing products that are likely to be raised? Get properly briefed on this by the people in closest contact with the customer so that you don't blunder into a minefield. You should collect any information you may need to support your case (such as sales figures over the previous year) and you should certainly consider Stage 3, i.e. in what order to present the material. If, for instance, there is a critical service issue buzzing around, do you raise this at the start of the meeting and get it out of the way or do you risk ignoring it? If you do the latter and the subject is brought up right at the end by the customer and the discussion becomes heated, then it may sour a potential sale. Even if you don't write down the exact words you intend to use in a face-to-face meeting, at least consider how to present the information in such a way as to make the most compelling impact.

For broader occasions, Stage 1 of your preparation should consist of a general free-thinking session in which you just note any thoughts you have, however wild they may be at this stage; surprisingly, they will often be your best ideas (perhaps because the adrenalin may be flowing at the time if you are charged up by receiving the invitation). The random points need not be detailed. If you are reviewing the coming year just note 'new depot Eastern' to remind you to talk about the challenge you will all face with the opening of the new depot in Norwich. Similarly, 'Smith's launch ABC 3rd Qtr' will be a reminder to mention how the introduction of a new product in the third quarter by a major rival will clearly affect your affairs.

Next, move to Stage 2 and start collecting supporting information. If this involves detailed research that will take time then put it in hand straight away. If the function is some weeks away there may be a tendency to put things off; resist the temptation. Incidentally, when you are assembling facts and figures to support a case (and you may end up with quite a file of material), do *not* be tempted to shade or distort such information because someone in your audience is sure to know better and if they challenge you in a question-and-answer session they will destroy your credibility and devalue those parts of your message which are true. Obviously, you are not compelled to reveal damaging information if you feel you can get away without doing so — although it may be wiser to assume that bad news will out — but don't shade any marginal material.

While making your random notes and assembling back-up information, do keep in mind that it may sometimes be necessary to state the obvious. Association dinners often feature a review of the state of the particular industry by the chairman or president. Such rituals — boring though they may be — are difficult to avoid either because they are too deeply entrenched or because the purpose may be to reach a wider audience via the media. Whatever the reasons, such reviews rarely include much that is challenging or original, which is why in some companies lots are drawn to be the official representatives at such functions, with the *losers* having to attend.

If you have been asked to speak to a group and you don't know much about their field of interest, then use your own industry as a reference point to draw comparisons, e.g. 'I don't know much about bricks, but when making cabinets over half the energy we use...', etc., etc.

A small collection of books may help your preparation process. For instance, a thesaurus can be useful if you are trying to construct deft turns of phrase and want a change of vocabulary, although you should resist trying so hard for alliteration that your sentences become twee or tortuous. A dictionary and, perhaps, an encyclopaedia may be worth having, while if you wish to quote from the Bible — and there is no reason why you should not do so if it is appropriate and in good taste — a concordance will guide you to suitable quotes on most subjects.

ASSEMBLING THE MATERIAL

Again, you may develop your own methods, but I think it is worth scribbling all your thoughts, plus any quotations or supporting information, onto cards, of roughly postcard size; many printers will be happy to sell you offcuts. Use one card for each point you wish to make so that it will be easy to shuffle the running order as you prepare your first draft. If you have, say, sheaves of market research just jot 'market research' on a card at this stage — you can extract the detail later.

Once you have assembled what you feel is enough material, you really need to grade your information according to what people *must* know, what they *should* know and, finally, what it would be nice for them to know but is by no means essential. To help the grading process it may be helpful to consider what questions the audience is likely to have about your topic, and then answer them in advance during your preparation. Evaluating the information will, above all, clarify your thinking and it will also help you if you have to delete material because you are over-running. At this point you could either colour code your rough note cards or put 1, 2, 3 or A, B, C on them according to the importance of the information.

Next, sort the cards into what appears to be a sensible running order; for example: an introduction;

an outline of what you plan to talk about; your key points, with arguments to support your case; maybe a brief note of any opposition view (being careful to demolish it, of course) or any difficult challenges being faced; then a summing up.

That's one suggested running order but the permutations are endless and — if you are remembering the advice to keep thinking of your audience — you will not fall into any stereotyped pattern but will vary your approach according to the occasion. There will be many occasions (for example, when proposing the toast to an association) where you would be unlikely to be citing opposition views. However, nothing says that all speeches have to be cosy and comfortable and if you were addressing, say, bankers you could certainly refer to the dramatic changes that have taken place in their world (perhaps if speakers at bankers' functions in the past had made such points the banks wouldn't have been caught quite so napping).

Whatever the occasion and whether or not you wish to be controversial, your card sorting (or whatever other system you use to build an address) must aim to make your speech *flow*, ideally with a theme to tie it all together; your audience will get confused if you bob about without any logical links, so you must have a thread running through your presentation. You may find you will sort your cards two or three times until you get them into the best order and, in the process, don't hesitate to delete points altogether — you should take care to avoid information overload.

When you are happy with the running order, go through and consider how to link the points together. Keep in mind that you are in effect telling a story, and I would stress again that it must flow;

random facts in themselves may be interesting but placed end to end without any link they may simply become confusing. Still using your rough cards at this stage, either put extra ones into your pack or scribble additional, linking, comments on the existing cards, e.g. 'That's the home market, now let's look at exports'. Such 'signposts' between sections will help you carry the audience with you because people are happier when they know what is going on.

Add extra cards to your 'pack' if necessary; one with an outline of your opening words will be important. Most business folk abhor wasting time so if, say, you are drafting your introductory remarks for a meeting you are hosting, your first card should remind you that having made them welcome you should tell them what is going to happen at the meeting; for instance: 'Roger will talk about our new product then June, who has just joined us from ABC Ltd, will tell you about the plans to market the range'. If guests are present from another department or another company, then jot a note to make them welcome. Don't worry about the actual words you will use at this stage in your preparation — concentrate on getting the points you plan to make into the best order.

If you are going to involve your audience by inviting questions as you go along, jot this point on one of your first cards to remind you to say so.

Shock tactics may help you to gain attention at the start of a presentation, but I suppose you would still need care if saying 'I used to be a bank robber' before going on to sell life assurance. And although you should not waste people's time, don't put your key message too early in a speech or presentation; let the meeting settle down first. A few common courtesies — hope you had a good journey, welcome to our friends from the Northern division or whatever — will give an audience time to settle. If, for example, you are talking about a brand new product you could spend a short time discussing market trends before going on to explain the relevance of your new offering.

THE KEY MESSAGE

When you come to the main point of your presentation, try to bring something fresh to it but remember that not everyone may want a highly technical approach. Have technical information on a product available of course, if relevant, and touch on the highlights but if, for example, you are trying to promote a new air-conditioning system to a general audience, details of cost and ease of operation may be more important than a technical lecture on how it works. If you designed it yourself *you* may be deeply interested in this aspect; don't assume anyone else will be.

If there is a weakness in your case it may be less damaging to mention it yourself rather than wait for someone else to point it out, but do follow any comment with a strong plus point. Obviously, in grading your information you should have put all your plus points in the 'must know' category.

To strengthen a point you may decide to argue against it: 'It may be said that the changes will improve sales, but it can be argued that they will in fact destroy them because.... However, don't labour the point and avoid too much of 'on the one hand...on the other'. The audience wants to hear *your* views, so sooner rather than later you should put them across. Positively.

Do make sure the audience grasps your key message: don't wrap it up so cosily that no one spots it, or cloud a message just because it is a sad one. Don't, for instance, waffle on about the benefits to a field-force of this or that if the real crux is that you are downgrading their company cars.

Having considered your main message, move on to draft your final section. You may say, 'So let me sum up' and then repeat your key points, while on the day, if you can think on your feet, you should re-state anything which you felt was misunderstood or which got an adverse reaction; for instance, 'I know you groaned when I mentioned the new discount structure, well, let me just remind you that...'.

If you recap on your main points, it may help to rephrase some of them to introduce a fresh line, although if you have a slogan to put across then obviously you should not tamper with it. Don't forget to make a note to thank people where appropriate — perhaps a conference organizer, chairman or chef.

Having finished the notes for your concluding section, take one final detached look at the whole thing, remembering the earlier point that your message is not what you think you have said but what your audience takes away with them. If people cannot understand something they have read they can look at it again, but they have only one chance with the spoken word; if you haven't assembled your thoughts properly you have little chance of being understood. Remember too the importance of having a logical flow to it all.

Now you have sorted your facts into a logical order you can give some thought to the actual *words* you will use to put them across (we'll cover how to remember them all in a later chapter). Try to aim for authority rather than superiority — give your audience the feeling that you know what you are doing and are therefore a suitable person to be addressing them, but don't patronize them. Avoid the use of too many superlatives or you may sound complacently self-satisfied. As a general rule, use words you will feel comfortable with and, more important, that your audience will feel comfortable with.

If you have some boring but nevertheless essential facts to put across, warn your audience that it may be heavy going for a moment: 'I am sorry to give you so many figures but unless we clearly understand how the market for our product is shifting, we cannot hope to increase penetration next year'. Except for specialist audiences you should avoid complicated figures or statistics, although keep in mind that a whole number, such as 9 per cent, may look like an estimate whereas 9.1 per cent seems somehow more accurate. It may be wise to avoid hostages to fortune by understating, rather than overstating, such things as sales objectives: nicer in a year's time to be able to say you beat your target rather than just missed it. If you boast in January that you are going to climb to second behind the industry giant and you finish third, you will be seen to have failed come December; if you say you hope to get into the top six, third will be seen as a success. Same result, different affect on morale through more sensible pre-planning.

Avoid scattering so many statistics about that people lose your thread and, where possible, add word pictures to bring statistics to life — while quoting the number of cases of baked beans sold, say 'enough to fill the Albert Hall three times'. Such illustrations should not be patronizing or too familiar. The same applies if a celebrity is present. If you say that 'Fred was a gold medallist' and they all know that, you may mildly irritate them; better to mention it with a passing comment like 'Of course, when Fred here won his gold medal, we were still selling..'.

Try not to be stuffy: you may be deeply interested in the minutiae of your subject, and so may your employees, but don't assume others will be or you may have to fight to hold their attention. And don't pretend to be more knowledgeable than you really are because you won't be too audible if you talk through your hat.

A lot of 'don'ts', I know, but don't string a series of platitudes and clichés together and expect it to move people. It won't. And don't pose. Be yourself and don't talk up or down to an audience. And keep in mind that too even a pace can be monotonous so try to vary things if you can; you could insert a card with a reminder to lighten things at a particular point with a witticism.

Admitting your mistakes, perhaps to illustrate a point, may liven things up — at least the audience will warm to you because you will seem that much more human. It helps too to involve your audience whenever you can. For example: 'Your sales in this division last year equalled those in the whole of Scandinavia'. Actual examples and case studies will hold attention better than generalities, so use them when you can.

Although you should be as natural as possible when speaking, you may still need to move into a higher gear and give more thought to your actual choice of words than for normal conversation; after all, you are to some extent putting on a performance. George Bush talked about 'a thousand points of light' in one speech and admitted he didn't know what on earth it meant but thought it sounded good. You may not choose to go to such extreme lengths but do at least think about the actual phrases you will use. Occasionally, try to add a rhythm, perhaps 'a rhythm of three': 'we are going to do this, we are going to do that and we are going to do the other'. But watch that your attempts to add rhythm don't turn your speech into a sing-song or poem; it must sound natural. As an alternative you could repeat a key word or phrase: 'We will face the challenge of A, we will face the challenge of B, we will face the challenge of C'.

Incidentally, if you decide to refer to personalities when speaking, do choose people relevant to your audience. If you are addressing a young group and refer to actors, sporting stars or other public figures long dead they may wonder who on earth you are talking about. Conversely, if you try to be desperately modern by referring to current pop stars, then do take proper advice so that you deliver an apt reference, otherwise you may just make yourself look a bit silly.

ADDRESSING A FOREIGN AUDIENCE

Finally, if you are to speak to a foreign audience, find someone of that nationality to steer you clear of the obvious pitfalls and to introduce you to their customs. Obviously, you should delete any very topical references or comments, such as those about domestic television programmes, because they won't be understood, and you must be careful not to patronize foreigners. You and I may know that our country is best but it is a bit tactless to let them know that we know.

Recognize the fact that, while foreigners in your audience may not speak or understand your language fluently, they may be reluctant to say so. It is up to you to slow the pace and, for instance, take the trouble to explain any unusual words or phrases which you are forced to use (obviously you should stick to basic words as far as possible).

It may be that you have the luxury of an interpreter. If so, do practise together and break up your material into clear sections so that one thought or point at a time can be translated. Bear in mind that this process will double the length of your speech. Address the audience not the interpreter when speaking, by the way.

Even if you do have an interpreter you should practise, and then say, a few words of welcome to guests in their language, perhaps going on to explain why an interpreter is being used. If you are confident, you may even tackle an entire speech in a language you don't actually speak. Write your words in English, then ask a national of the group you will be addressing to translate them and say them into a tape recorder for you. Now write a phonetic interpretation of exactly what is on the tape. This interpretation can look like total gibberish, provided you can follow the notes and they sound like the foreign language when you say them. Then rehearse. I followed exactly this method for a 15-minute speech in a language I don't speak and was later congratulated on my excellent accent, so it seems to work. Incidentally, it is perhaps worth finding a national with a fairly neutral accent to make the tape for you — think how hilarious but perhaps distracting it could be for, say, a non-

English-speaking German to make a speech in England by this method if it had been recorded for him by a broad Scot.

Note: This chapter has assumed that you are writing your speech or presentation yourself. Senior executives often have the luxury of having their words written for them (some companies retain or commission full-time speech writers). This is all very comforting but the person standing up and coping with the humiliation will be you if it all goes wrong, so you must take an interest in what you are going to say by, for instance, briefing the writer properly; you must believe in what you are saying (how are you going to convince people if you don't?) and you must fine tune the words so that you feel comfortable with them. Don't pick up a binder, walk to the podium and, from the way you stumble when reading the words, make it all too obvious that it is the first time you've seen them. The worst sin of all is not to take any trouble beforehand, sense things going wrong when you are on your feet and then make some facetious crack about 'I didn't write this stuff, of course'. All you are doing is insulting your audience and making yourself look an idiot.

CHECKLIST 3

- [ ] What sort of character will you be perceived to be?
- [ ] Make general notes on your topic. Use scrap cards.
- [ ] Any controversial issues to be faced or avoided?
- [ ] Do you need to state the obvious?
- [ ] Collect supporting information. Don't shade it.
- [ ] Will opposing views strengthen your case if quoted, then rebuffed?
- [ ] What questions will the audience want your speech to answer?
- [ ] Sort your material.
- [ ] Grade information according to importance.
- [ ] Write your words.
- [ ] Make your key messages clear.
- [ ] Strive for a 'flow'.
- [ ] Build in signposts.
- [ ] Beware jargon, abbreviations, statistics.
- [ ] Don't create hostages to fortune when making, for example, sales forecasts.

☐ Plan your closing remarks.

☐ Have a final re-think. Do your words meet your objectives and will they meet your audience's expectations?

☐ If your speech is written for you by someone else, check and fine tune it.

☐ **Foreign audiences**
- Avoid topical domestic references.
- Guard against giving offence.
- Slow the pace if they are not totally *au fait* with your language.
- Liaise closely with any interpreter.
- Say at least a few words in the foreign language/s.

4
TALKS, LECTURES AND SPECIAL OCCASIONS

As a business person, not all your talking is likely to be from a podium to a captive in-house audience — you may also be asked to give talks on business affairs to outside groups. Such opportunities should be seized because they can be a useful way of promoting your company; if you give a good lecture to a local school, for instance, you may encourage bright youngsters to join your company. However, you need to prepare perhaps even more carefully when talking to outside groups than to your colleagues because, if things go wrong, you can do more damage to your reputation and that of your company.

It all comes back yet again to audience analysis, because it's important to make an apt speech to an outside group. If, as 'the leading local business executive', you are presenting prizes at a school don't drone on for half an hour about the minutiae of your business otherwise you will bore everyone senseless and, worse, drive even more kids into the arts rather than industry. And don't make the youngsters squirm by turning up in your grey business suit and then trying to be desperately hip, unless you can deliberately send yourself up with style in the process.

Keep in mind with outside groups that abbreviations and even percentages may not always be understood; talk about 7 out of 10 people rather than 70 per cent. Ruthlessly cut out 'business-speak' or meaningless 'filler' words planted in a forlorn attempt to make you appear erudite. Sadly, business often stands rightly accused of obfuscating and using absurd phrases — 'human resources management', 'at this point in time', 'run it up the flag and see who salutes' — the list is endless. This does nothing to make communication easier; what it does do is make industrialists look pompous and silly to their broader audience and, of course, it also hands ammunition to newspaper columnists who like to send up business people.

With that advice in mind, let us now look at some of the specific occasions on which you may be called upon to speak.

There is relatively little difference between *talks* and *lectures*, but talks are likely to be given to those who are interested in a subject, however mildly, or have asked you to talk about your business because they have a hole in their social calendar to fill; lectures are more likely to be directed at those who already know something about a subject and want, or need, to know more. Lectures may be more formal and are expected to inform more than talks, which may be quite general; both perhaps appeal more to the intellect than to the emotions (as would be the case in a public speech).

It follows that if you are to deliver a talk or lecture you need to know your subject. Anyone can propose a toast to a business association because anyone can dig up a few things to say before asking people to raise their glasses, but not everyone can, or should, stand and talk or lecture on nuclear fission. You should not talk or lecture without a reasonable knowledge of your subject because, if you've only read a couple of books and try to bluff your way through, Sod's Law states that there will be someone far more knowledgeable in the audience who will be itching to air his or her knowledge by asking you questions (something you are usually protected from when making pure business presentations or public speeches).

It will help you to strike the right note if you know what has gone before your pitch, either on the day or at the previous function held by the body. If you know one of the previous speakers to the group you are due to address, contact him or her to find out at what level you need to pitch things. (Organizers should be warned that speakers 'on the circuit' swap notes and chairpeople who get drunk or let things get out of control — or sometimes both — quickly become known.)

Scientific bodies often like to have lectures submitted well in advance; in fact, I believe the undignified scrambles by learned people to get papers 'published' (so that they can list them on their CVs) and the squeals if theirs are not chosen are often funnier than any after-dinner speaker could be. Some associations issue papers and then members sit politely while they are read through. I know there are many groups — especially international bodies where people need time for translation and contemplation — where such things are necessary, but resist it if there appears to be no sensible reason. The chances of anything being sparkling and original if it is weeks old are remote. If you are faced with reading a paper that everyone has in front of them, I think I'd still throw in the odd ad lib, if for no other reason than to keep them, and you, awake.

Moving on from talks and lectures, for the businessman or woman *annual general meetings* really call for as much organizational and legal skill as expertise at speaking because the venue, refreshments served (if any) and, above all, attention to the rulebook are almost as important as the words. An AGM is one occasion when you should probably not attempt to entertain or ad lib, but should simply concentrate on grinding through the business in hand. Keep in mind that the efficiency with which you conduct the meeting as well as your manner during it (confident, too cocksure, hangdog or whatever) can send out very powerful signals to shareholders and the financial pundits.

Sadly, in an increasingly strident world, your AGM may become something of a *protest meeting*, or you may need to protest yourself, for example if you are leading a group of fellow traders campaigning for or against something. If you are the person faced with the protests, try not to lose your temper and try not to create martyrs by, for instance, ejecting people who may be trying to raise a point which the majority feel is fairly valid. If you yourself are leading a lobbying group then don't prepare your words in isolation. You may be the spokesperson for your group, but the planting of questions to be thrown at 'unfriendly' speakers or officials should be carefully planned in advance, as should the preparation of any banners to be waved and any stunts. Yes, stunts — in the weird media world in which we live, you may, reluctantly, have to resort to such things to get attention. French farmers seem singularly successful with such methods.

Retirement parties or presentations can cause a disproportionate amount of embarrassment, perhaps because, although they feature people who work together every day, they can become somewhat stilted and awkward. If you are scheduled to make a presentation and someone has worked for the company for a long time, do them the courtesy of giving proper thought to what to say, no matter how inundated you are with business problems. You may, cynically, think it doesn't matter if you are casual and indifferent because Arthur's retiring to Eastbourne anyway — but what about the effect on all your other employees who see you as uncaring?

Be as natural as possible (unless of course the natural you is not a particularly pleasant person, in which case try to inject a little warmth into the occasion) and recall one or two incidents that have happened to the retiree over the years which will amuse and at the same time serve to show what fine colleagues they have been. Keep in mind that the younger members of staff won't be able to follow laborious tales about things that happened years ago. If retirees' spouses are with them, pay them proper tribute, too. Incidentally, the handing over of jokey presents — along with more conventional ones — is usually a happy feature of retirement presentations. Kissograms and the like are also occurring more often but instigators need to keep in mind that such 'happenings' can sometimes get out of hand and cause general unease. Beware!

If you are the person who is retiring, you may feel a retirement party is time to let off steam and deliver a few home truths to management — you will check that your pension plan is fireproof first, won't you?

Not too soon after retirement presentations I hope, you may have to speak at the *funeral* of an old employee or colleague. Perhaps more than ever, these are times when you must have a proper 'feel' for the occasion — you could blunder if, say, you were unaware that a distraught woman was a mistress, not a wife. In some places it is traditional to deliver panegyrics to the departed; on other occasions it may be appropriate to tell jokes, or certainly anecdotes, at memorial services for well-known or particularly well-loved people — if it is done well. Speeches will sometimes be called for at the gatherings that follow funerals; it may even be appropriate to mention that a memorial fund of some sort is to be started.

If you are required to do any of the above then prepare very carefully, use tact and be sincere.

If you are called upon to propose a *vote of thanks*, perhaps to a speaker at a trade association meeting, try to stay awake, listen to what the speaker says and then mention one or two points to show that you were paying attention. Don't go on too long in proposing a vote of thanks — it is really only a trigger for a second round of applause, anyway. Even if you disagree with most of what the speaker said, you should not launch into a major speech putting the counter-view but instead say something about how 'thought-provoking' the speech was and then (maybe) either put one or two key opposing points or correct blatant errors in what was said. You don't have to be obsequious if the speaker was totally at odds with the audience, but do at least be polite.

If you are involved in organizing a business meeting you may sometimes have to act as *toastmaster* or *master of ceremonies*. If so, ensure that you are properly briefed on what is to happen. When and if you have to announce something, such as a change of venue, then pitch up your voice to command attention, while if you have to introduce, say, a cabaret be enthusiastic so that you shift the mood of the audience up a gear. Above all, it may be a key task to get people to be quiet and ready to listen to a speaker or an entertainer.

If making presentations at a *prizegiving* you may only be expected to murmur 'congratulations' to each of the prize-winners as they collect their awards. If more is expected — such as a state-of-the-nation address before or after an awards ceremony — do make your words relevant to the occasion and the audience. It may, of course, be entirely appropriate to turn awards ceremonies for salesforces into fairly ribald affairs with over-the-top trumpet fanfares and 'cod' prizes following the serious ones. Sometimes the latter can carry more than a little bite — I was once asked to present a 'Home Sweet Home' sampler to a sales executive and only found out later that the laughter, while friendly, was because he was bottom of the sales league, possibly because of time spent at a second home abroad!

If called upon to *open a fête* (don't laugh, it's been known for business people to do so, although it usually signifies that everyone else approached has said 'no') then remember that your audience won't want to stand on the wet grass while you plough through several pages. Simply use sincere words in pushing the cause for which the affair is being held and then declare it open in ringing tones. The tones may be more ringing than you had intended, because an outdoor public address system is not exactly the speaker's best friend — try to check it in advance, though it may do you little good. After you've declared the thing open, you'd better trot round and show some interest in the stalls. If a press photographer wants a shot of you in action, choose an activity which is not too undignified — bowling for a pig is perhaps better than looking like one as you stuff yourself at the cake stall.

If, instead of a fête, you are *opening a new building*, try to dig up some appropriate point to lighten the proceedings — as well as talking about the size and the export potential that will result mention, say, that it is built on the site of a notorious robbers' hideout ('...and nothing has changed').

Increasingly, business executives get roped into *fundraising*. If you have to make a speech for a good cause then liaise closely with the organizer so that you are on your feet at the most propitious moment — for example, people are likely to donate more when they have had a glass or two of wine. Tell people what you are raising funds for and why; this is one occasion when you really should not read a speech because, to be effective, an 'appeal' should be from the heart. If there are tax advantages for your audience through covenants then say so and, if you plan an auction to raise funds, approach one or two key supporters beforehand and ask them to start the ball rolling. I don't know about you but I find such auctions are often deeply embarrassing, with either a lack of bids or a couple of drunks bidding ludicrous amounts for tat.

If you are hoping to climb the political ladder as a businessman or woman, I am sure you won't need any advice from me about *political meetings*. However, if you are attending one in the hope of asking questions (perhaps on an issue that affects your company), then position yourself where you can be seen and speak in a clear voice. Don't turn your question into a long speech because the audience will react against you and most hardened politicians will have well-used put-downs with which they will respond.

Apart from the AGM, the most fraught meeting, for the business executive may be a *press conference*. Dealing with the media does need care. Above all, vow not to waste journalists' time — consider whether your message could be put across just as well via a press release; your 20th or 25th anniversary may seem terribly important to you but don't expect the enthusiasm to be shared. If you do decide to invite journalists to a conference, avoid a long formal speech as such; instead, just outline the points you want to make and then invite questions. If you have a press release available and/or a copy of your speech (you should), then say so at the start to save journalists having to make notes. If your news is bad, then try to present it in as positive a way as possible ('the job cuts now will help to guarantee the remaining jobs for the future') but don't try deliberately to conceal the bad news — you will be caught out.

Competition among newspapers and magazines for sheer survival, coupled with aggressive interviewing techniques seen on television, may lead to reporters quizzing you harder than you expected; this may seem rather harsh when all you are doing is announcing a new workshop extension, but don't let such an approach rattle you. To concentrate the mind before a press conference, ask someone to throw at you the most awkward questions they can think of about your affairs so that you can rehearse or at least consider your answers. However, watch that such a run-through beforehand doesn't psyche you up so high that you assume all the journalists are hostile, because your replies to them may then be too sharp. I've seen one business executive so charged up by considering in advance all the awkward questions he might get that when greeted by 'good morning', he almost snapped 'what was wrong with yesterday?'

Keep in mind, at press conferences, that the best journalists may prefer to ask searching questions privately — if there are one or two such people who have a major influence on your industry because of the paper they write for, it will probably be worth while arranging separate sessions for them.

Don't say at a press conference that you 'expect' coverage — if your news isn't strong enough it won't get published. You have absolutely no divine right to be given coverage and implying that you expect it will simply irritate any journalists present (the decision whether or not a story appears will often not be in their hands, anyway).

If, after all your efforts, a report appears with mistakes in it, don't phone the editor to complain while you are in a rage — calm down and contemplate first because it may be better to let things lie. Demanding a published apology may prolong the coverage given to an issue and may flush out and into print opponents to your plans. Console yourself with the thought that few people remember what's printed anyway — without cheating, can you remember what the headline was in your newspaper yesterday? Of course you can't — so what impact is an obscure item on page seven likely to have? The best way of preventing errors is to have accurate press releases available.

Incidentally, you can so easily hit problems with the media that it's wise, whenever you are speaking, to check if journalists are present and, if they are and you are not sure of your relationship with them, guard against indiscretions you would not want to appear in print.

PROTOCOL

One thing that causes speakers a little concern when they are away from the purely business environment is the protocol of how people should be addressed. Although it is worth taking the trouble to get things right (if nothing else to avoid being seen as that oaf from industry), don't get into a nervous tangle over it because it is not a matter of life and death. As a broad guide, list key people roughly in their order of importance (bearing in mind that their feelings of self-importance may differ from your views). The head of a group or organization should be mentioned before everyone else except royalty. It is usual to add 'Mr' or 'Madam' to their position, e.g. 'Mr Chairman'. Personally, I find the word 'chairperson' grates and some people are not wild about 'chairwoman', but increasingly you will have to get your tongue round such words — ask the lady in question how she would like to be addressed.

On other occasions a toastmaster will usually know the form, while on one occasion I spoke at, a bright organizer gave all the speakers a slip with the correct preamble set out on it.

If you are asked to say *grace* before a formal meal, try to come up with something more original than 'For what we are about to receive may the Lord make us truly thankful'. Without wishing to over-dramatize the saying of grace, it is usually the first thing said and if you can produce something apt and original you will get things off to a fine start. I once heard a clergyman say: 'Bless the chef and all who serve us; from indigestion Lord preserve us', after which everyone sat down smiling. In striving to be original, it is acceptable to say something like: 'Bless our food, our friendship and the aims of our association' but don't stray too far in this direction, and on no account plug a product or ask people to pray for the downfall of your key competitor (fervently though you may wish for this).

If, later in the meal, you are asked to propose the *loyal toast*, no speech is required, in fact one would be quite wrong; just say: 'The Queen'. The master of ceremonies, toastmaster or chair should ask guests to 'be upstanding' before the loyal toast is proposed. Patriotic guests may occasionally wish to sing the national anthem after the loyal toast but this is rare — mercifully so, because the result is usually acutely embarrassing.

There is no formal or legal connection between the loyal toast and smoking but it is usual for someone to say after the loyal toast that 'you have your chairman's permission to smoke' or, more likely, 'to carry on smoking'. More sarcastic comments are starting to be heard and it's going to be interesting to watch over the next few years how organizers handle the question of smoking — it won't be long before formal dinners have smoking and non-smoking sections just as delegates seated theatre-style for a conference have, or should have, a choice.

CHECKLIST 4

- [ ] Whatever the occasion, analyse and think of your audience.

- [ ] Jargon won't be understood by general audiences.

- [ ] **Talks and lectures**
    - [ ] Know what you are talking about.
    - [ ] How have previous speakers fared?
    - [ ] Avoid submitting texts weeks in advance.

- [ ] **AGMs**
    - [ ] Organizational and legal skills important.
    - [ ] Efficiency and manner in which you conduct an AGM 'says' something about your company.

- [ ] **Protest meetings**
    - [ ] Avoid creating martyrs if protested against.
    - [ ] If protesting, plan your total campaign.

- [ ] **Retirements**
    - [ ] Make an effort.
    - [ ] If retiring, check your pension is foolproof before sounding off.
    - [ ] Kissograms are often embarrassing for all concerned.

- [ ] **Funerals**
    - [ ] Must have a proper 'feel' for the occasion.
    - [ ] Don't rule out humour.

- [ ] **Vote of thanks**
    - [ ] Stay awake.
    - [ ] Refer to one or two points the speaker made.
    - [ ] Don't make a long speech putting counter-views.

- [ ] **Toastmaster/master of ceremonies**
    - [ ] Be properly briefed.
    - [ ] Exude confidence.
    - [ ] Pitch up your voice.

- [ ] **Prizegivings**
    - [ ] Again, analyse your audience.
    - [ ] Don't make yourself look silly by striving to be 'with it' with a young audience.

- [ ] **Fêtes**
    - [ ] Assume public address will be poor outdoors, so no long speeches.

- [ ] **Fundraising**
    - [ ] Must be sincere and clearly believe in the cause.
    - [ ] Consider timing: people will be more generous after drinks.
    - [ ] Highlight any tax advantages for donors.

- [ ] **Press conferences**
    - [ ] Is your conference really necessary?
    - [ ] Prepare properly, e.g. consider the questions you are likely to face.
    - [ ] Minutiae of your industry may bore people.
    - [ ] Assume bad news will out.
    - [ ] Don't imply you 'expect' media coverage.
    - [ ] Don't overact if coverage is inaccurate.

5
HAVE YOU HEARD THE ONE ABOUT...?

Let's face it, business life isn't all Concorde trips and megabuck deals; at times it can be mind-bendingly boring. And never more so than when listening to a long drawn-out business presentation. So, if you are due to make a presentation or speech, should you use humour to lighten it? The answer is a qualified 'yes'. Qualified because while laughter will relax an audience and help people to stay awake, you will be more at risk if you decide to use humour. If, during a speech or presentation, you make a particular point about your business you will not be seeking an immediate reaction, although you may be hoping to change minds and you may even get a few nods of agreement. If, however, you introduce a witty one-liner or tell an elaborate joke then you *are* seeking a clear response — you hope the audience will smile or laugh and, if they don't, you have to a certain extent 'failed' and equally the audience has to a certain extent 'failed' you — all of which can cause a slightly uneasy air. I don't know about you, but if a series of jokes by a speaker fails, I want to crawl under the table with embarrassment even though I'm not directly involved.

As there is an element of risk involved, you will be relieved to know that you don't *have* to use humour in a presentation and, in fact, if you know in your heart that you haven't got the ability — that all-important 'timing' — to use humour, then don't do so. And however analytical you may be in your general approach to business, don't attempt to overanalyse humour. Life is too short.

An occasional lighthearted touch that produces inward chuckles even if not gales of laughter will certainly help to freshen a presentation and a touch of humour may open ears and minds to more serious messages. So consider using it if possible but if you've got doubts then use wit (such as a quote from Mark Twain) rather than more bludgeoning humour, such as a long joke. A specific joke sends out a clear signal that a laugh is expected at the end. This has all the dangers mentioned a moment ago — you won't be seeking quite such a positive response from a witty one-liner and can glide straight on to your next sentence if you don't get a chuckle. The size of the audience may influence what, if any, humour you use. If the audience is small there may not be sufficient critical mass to make humour really successful. This chapter is called 'Have you heard the one about...' because those words, if they preface a tale that everyone *has* heard, are the most chilling an audience can hear. Well, perhaps not the most chilling — 'that reminds me of the story of...' comes very close because such stories are rarely apt, they are invariably too complicated and they always drag on too long. Not many people are thrilled to hear 'here's a good one' either. If you overpersist in joke-telling you may detract from what else you have to say; worse, you may be typecast as the 'company clown' and be expected to fill that role for ever more, and what that may do to your career prospects won't be any joke at all. Humour should only be used if it is relevant. If it isn't, it will make you as the deliverer seem irrelevant too.

Source Material

Despite the awful warnings, if you decide to use humour, where do you find the material? Well, many books of jokes are available but they do need care: they may feature tired material and it is very difficult to tell from the printed page whether the material will work or be right for you. A joke must suit you and you must feel comfortable when telling it. As an example, a company accountant might feel or look foolish telling a story more clearly suitable for a hearty sales executive. If you do feel comfortable with a story, telling it may actually help to relax you. Don't try to wade through joke books at one sitting or you will get indigestion; read a few pages at a time and consider whether something can be adapted for your purpose. More fertile territory than joke books may be books of quotations, because you will almost certainly find something to suit any occasion and if you say 'As Oscar Wilde said...' and then use a quotation, well, if it doesn't get a reaction then to some extent it may seem as much Oscar's fault as yours. Remember that humour often comes from the unexpected with an audience led to expect one thing and then given another. Never use a joke that needs explaining, by the way.

Collect clippings from newspapers and magazines of things that amuse you; you can rest assured most people will have forgotten them if you use them in a few weeks' time. For the same reason, old jokes may work perfectly well (which perhaps explains why viewing figures for TV comedy repeats are so high).

You could even try writing something amusing yourself. Yes, you could — a reference to a well-known character in the company will not have to be very inspired to get a laugh. For a relaxed company occasion it may not be difficult to write a parody of a popular song or television programme, using references to company people, but, if you do, don't make them too long; better to leave people wanting more than yawning.

A few general points on humour:

- ☐ The occasion will influence how much, if any, humour you should use. In general, after-dinner speeches should feature humour more than formal presentations where there is more information to be put across. A string of jokes at a meeting with a serious intent will become tiresome.
- ☐ Tailor jokes to suit you or the occasion where possible — this will make them more relevant to your audience.
- ☐ Steer clear of long complicated jokes. You are more likely to get them wrong; people's agony will be prolonged if they have heard them before or you tell them badly, and if you 'die' in telling a long joke you will die in a big way and your speech may perish too. Crisp one-line comments are much safer.
- ☐ Avoid 'competing' with jokes. If a previous speaker from another department uses humour successfully, you don't *have* to try to cap him.
- ☐ Do appreciate that an audience needs to be at ease before they can laugh — if they are waiting for a message about redundancies, they won't want to waste time listening to jokes. In fact, at such times, humour can get a very negative reaction.
- ☐ Topical references should be topical. At the start of one of his shows Barry Humphries had an

elaborate warm-up slide presentation with a good joke about a politician. When the show opened the joke was topical and immediately appreciated; nearly a year later I saw the show again and this time there was a pause before the laugh and you could sense the audience trying to recall the incident referred to before laughing. References should not be *too* immediate, mind — if you hear something on a 7 p.m. news bulletin as you are driving to a function, don't assume everyone will understand a joke about it at 7.30 p.m.

☐ Be cautious in ribbing the cherished traditions of a group you are addressing unless you can do so very affectionately.

☐ Don't be put off by the thought that you may be out of touch because you don't understand all this talk of 'alternative comedy'. Humour is humour and, while some fringe comedy is very funny, much simply consists of using four-letter words at full volume.

☐ If you are under attack on an issue there may be occasions when you should consider using humour against yourself (as Ronald Reagan did so effectively). Don't think it will always work though — eschew the jokes if you are facing environmental protestors or angry investors worrying about what you've done with their money.

☐ The timing of the occasion is important if you intend to joke about a well-known public figure (you can consider you have 'arrived' when comedians start to joke about you). As an example, jokes about Edwina Currie were well-received (even when they were rather cruel) when she was a high-profile politician. However, within

24 hours of her losing office over the salmonella scare, public sympathy swung behind her and cruel jokes during that period would have been inappropriate. At that point the government and the National Farmers Union became much easier targets and I heard an executive get a round of applause and laughter when he said 'We were hoping to get government compensation for the batch of faulty nuts and bolts we produced... but sadly the NFU would not let us become members'. And that illustrates my earlier point that topical references don't have to be brilliant to be funny. And if by the time this book appears you have forgotten Edwina Currie and salmonella, it also illustrates another earlier point — people forget quickly.

If timing is important when considering if it is appropriate to refer to people in the news, it is even more important when actually telling jokes or using humour. Try to learn by your own experiences and judge whether, if you get a laugh, you should cut in and carry on (which will bring some laughter to an early end) or wait until it all dies down, which could mean that those who stopped laughing first have been waiting with their attention flagging for you to resume. On such occasions the brighter people are likely to have got the point and laughed first and therefore be waiting for something new.

Accept that a joke will fail occasionally because another speaker has told it or it has been well used in the area or, even, because your timing is slightly off. A millisecond in the timing of a joke can make a significant difference — and I suspect such timing has to be born, although practise can improve almost anyone. If a joke does fail, try not to be thrown off your stride. It's not the end of the world, although if your managing director has stormed out I suppose you'd better start dusting off your CV.

I don't want to make you neurotic about using humour but you do need to be more alert; for instance, you need to consider the boundaries of good taste. An occasional 'bloody' for emphasis is unlikely to induce the vapours in an audience nowadays, but I don't think you should use four-letter words, no matter how common they have become on television. You need to be careful in using religious or ethnic jokes too. Humour with foreign audiences? Why not? The most nationalities I've addressed — successfully I immodestly add — at one sitting was 27 (at an international conference) and my only advice is simply to pay more attention to your preparation than ever, deleting purely domestic references — such as to television programmes — which will not be widely understood.

The success of using humour with a foreign audience may depend on whether their language has the subtlety for understatement, which forms the basis of a lot of humour. English humour seems to travel well with 'Fawlty Towers' and the Benny Hill programmes popular in most countries, while it appears that every nation jokes about another or parts of a country rib another. English v. Irish; Swedes v. Norwegians; Romans v. Milanese (in Italy anyone who wears a uniform is a target for humour); Walloons v. the Flemish and so on. And so on. And vice versa in every case.

So go ahead and use humour with a foreign audience. If you have any doubts, play safe and rib your own country rather than a foreign one.

Checklist 5

☐ You don't *have* to use humour — don't, if you know it's not really you.

☐ Size of audience may affect use of humour.

☐ An audience has to be at ease with itself to laugh.

☐ Don't joke if the audience knows bad news is coming.

☐ More risk with long jokes than witty one-liners.

☐ Topical references, e.g. to colleagues, may not need to be very funny to get a good reaction.

☐ Tailor humour so that it is relevant to you and/or your topic.

☐ Beware of becoming the 'company clown'.

☐ Collect newspaper clips of things that amuse.

☐ People have short memories.

☐ Avoid four-letter words.

☐ Humour *can* work with foreign audiences.

6
REMEMBERING THE WORDS

On many occasions when you have to speak there will be no problem in remembering what to say because you will be delivering the words standing at a lectern and reading a text housed in a binder. However, foolproof though this system should be, it still needs care. Above all, make sure that the words are written (or, more likely and desirably, typed) to be *said* not read. When speaking, people abbreviate 'it is' to 'it's' and 'that is' to 'that's'; so should you when having a speech typed.

You may get a more flowing presentation if you 'say' rather than 'dictate' (which may be too formal) your words into a tape recorder; do so working from the rough note cards referred to earlier. Next, get someone to type *exactly* what you have said — grammatical mistakes, split infinitives et al. Then go through this first draft and delete any silly phrases that have crept in, like 'at this point in time' if you mean 'now', and check that an over-efficient typist hasn't formalized your 'it's' into 'it is' and so on — you must keep the abbreviated versions if a speech is to sound natural. The point of using a tape recorder is to prepare a text to be said, not marked as part of an English grammar exam. Guard against over-long sentences but otherwise don't try to tidy up your draft too much or it may become stilted.

Typing should be at least double spaced and ideally should be in upper and lower case because capital letters throughout can be tiring to read. If you sometimes need spectacles for close work it may be worth considering a typewriter with a large typeface for your words so that you can keep eye contact with your audience without spectacles. Alternatively, you could make a feature of your spectacles, using them as something of a theatrical prop — putting them on to read a section as an indication of its importance, for instance. Or you could perhaps add a mild air of eccentricity by using a lorgnette or monocle. Whatever you do, though, don't over-use such things to the point that they irritate or distract an audience from your message.

If you do a lot of speaking you may consider putting your key comments onto a word processor, selecting sections for particular speeches, but be careful that this doesn't make your speeches sound stale and sterile.

Have enough words on each page of text to avoid constantly having to turn over; in time you will get to know that so many words equals so many minutes at your normal delivery rate. Don't go right to the bottom of a page or an audience will spend much of its time looking at the top of your head as you peer down. Watch that you don't break a sentence at the end of a page — if you have to turn over when you are delivering your key message it may disturb your flow and your audience's attention. If you turn over two pages by mistake and have to correct yourself you will lose a little of the audience's attention and the error will, of course, reinforce the fact that you are simply reading the words. I've even heard one presentation where the speaker turned over two pages by mistake and didn't notice...and neither did the audience.

Needless to say, pages of text should be carefully numbered — consider doing this at first in pencil so that you can modify the numbers if you have to insert additional sheets; better to do this than have pages 6A, 7B or whatever.

You may decide to have a stack of loose sheets of text, simply moving them from one pile to another after reading them, but this can be risky (the dangers of their getting out of order or falling on the floor are obvious) and it is better to keep a text in a binder. One with four rings will give better support than two but do check that the rings close properly to avoid pages snagging as you turn them. It is even worth trying to find a binder in which the rings open and close without a loud snap — the noise can be irritating if, say, you have to re-arrange your text while a previous speaker is in full cry. And do have a binder thick enough to house your text comfortably plus, perhaps, any supporting documents you may wish to refer to during a question and answer session; if a binder is crammed the rings may burst open and the text spill out. Trivial points? Maybe, but I don't think time spent on preparation is ever wasted and nor would you if, like me, you'd seen a poor devil stranded at a podium with two copies of page four in a binder instead of pages four and five. Such elementary errors, while they can usually be laughed off, don't exactly signal that you are an efficient executive, do they?

CUEING SYSTEMS

As a step up from reading from sheaves of paper, cueing systems are increasingly being used. With these you can look at your audience through one or more sheets of glass while you read the words, which are typed onto a paper roll then projected up and onto the glass in front of you by someone off stage (hopefully at the right pace for you). This method is much better for eye contact than putting your head down to read a speech, although fluffs can look somewhat strange. Exactly the same points apply about 'it's' and 'that's' when having the roll typed, of course, and although such cueing systems are reliable it is perhaps still worth having a spare copy of your words near at hand in case the system should fail.

Incidentally, if, instead of a cueing system mounted near the lectern, you are on a stage and using a large screen set some way in front of you to show you the words, check that the screen isn't reflected in any mirrors behind you — I have seen this happen a couple of times and on one occasion the speaker was thrown because an irreverent audience started chanting the words in unison with him!

Reading a presentation from a binder, sheaves of paper or cueing system will certainly be safe (easy, for instance, to cue in visual aids) but you will have to work hard to make the words sound natural. If you walk to a podium, plonk down a binder and read from it woodenly, you may be seen as just that — a plonker.

There may, of course, be times when a speech or a business presentation (or at least parts of one) may simply have to be read, for example if you are calling for specific and detailed government action on something, or if you have to acknowledge or thank a long list of people. And if you remain a hesitant speaker even after a lot of practise, then reading may be the best method for you. It will certainly place less strain on your nervous system.

BULLET POINTS

However, if you gain confidence in speaking, you will probably find it better to work from 'bullet points' — brief notes that remind you of what to say. This system is likely to make your speech or presentation more lively and natural than if you read it. If you intend to talk about market trends then a bullet saying '1st Quarter 26%, 2nd Quarter 28%' may be all you need to remind you what to say about how sales moved in the first half of the year. That bullet could be cut to '1Q:26, 2Q:28' or phrased in other ways — you will obviously develop your own shorthand system. Double or treble space the bullets so that there is room between them to add other notes if necessary as a meeting progresses.

If certain sections of a presentation need total accuracy then a partly written-out script, part bullet-point system may be more suitable. If so, I find it better to prepare a fresh set of notes rather than try to modify a fully typed speech — highlighting a few key words or phrases on a fully written-out text to use as bullet points may confuse you when you come to deliver your words.

Speaking entirely from brief bullet points will probably give you a more spontaneous approach than any other method. How detailed your bullets need to be will depend on your confidence and subject knowledge; if you pare your bullets down too far you may stumble once or twice in your first delivery; although your speech may actually seem sharper and more alive as a result. I often find if I prepare very scanty bullet points that I add more detailed comments to them just before I speak, simply through nerves. Incidentally, if you use bullet points it is advisable to prepare fresh notes rather than use the rough cards recommended for constructing your address.

You may develop a system of using capital letters for the key sections of your speech, with sub-headings to cover back-up points. Do whatever turns you on (note how silly such slang sounds — so avoid it when speaking) or, above all, calms you down.

The merits of using bullet points are even stronger if you have to give a speech rather than make a presentation, especially if the speech is to be given after a meal where a slightly less formal approach may be appropriate. But, again, if you are very hesitant then read it all rather than flounder.

You may feel that, instead of reading from a binder or autocue, or using bullet points, learning a speech or presentation by heart must be the most natural way of delivery, but it isn't and my advice is: *don't*. Memorizing everything is very hard work and unless you are a skilled actor your audience will still sense that you are 'reading' your speech, although in your mind rather than on a sheet of paper. And while it may seem the most spontaneous method, it isn't — losing your way can be fairly disastrous and, apart from anything else, you may be concentrating so hard on what you are going to say that it will be almost impossible for you to react to an audience or modify a point which another speaker covered earlier.

If you speak regularly on a subject with which you are totally familiar then you could, of course, speak without any memory aids at all; but speak spontaneously from the heart and don't attempt to memorize *exactly* what you are going to say. However, do remember any bits that go down well and use them again on future occasions. If you are using visual aids to support your presentation then it is even easier to use this method, because if you dry up you can move on to the next visual to remind you what to say. If you are using flipover charts you could lightly pencil bullet points on them (which the audience won't see) to remind you of the key things you want to mention about a particular chart or illustration.

If you have a fully written-out speech or work from bullet points, do use fairly firm paper, otherwise your every nervous tremble will be magnified. Don't worry about having notes on show (you don't need to colour key them to your suit or dress) but try not to have too many sheets — an audience may be just slightly hostile from the start if they suspect they face a marathon because of the volume of paper you have.

USING CARDS

If you make your notes on cards they should be small enough to go into a pocket or handbag yet big enough to be comfortable to hold. Cards *must* be numbered and ideally they should be held together with a string through holes punched in the top left-hand corners; if they are not connected then, sooner rather than later, you are going to drop them and they will get out of order.

Instead of using separate cards you may be able to get all your notes onto one card of A4 width (21 cm) and cut to about the same depth. If you fold such a sheet once you will have four columns, 10.5 cm wide and 21 cm deep, and the card will slip easily into a handbag or the inside pocket of a man's jacket. Start at the top of one column and write down your bullet points, then (remembering the point about turning at a convenient part of the speech) continue your bullets onto the second column. Choose a suitable point in your address to give yourself time to refold the card so that the inside columns are now on the outside ready to be used and then continue writing your bullets in columns three and four. Don't forget to number the columns, of course. Draw a line under your final note and then in any spare space jot down points which you could make if you have more time or if there is a questions session. You could also note on the card information such as the start time and address of the venue so that you have everything you need on the one document. Incidentally, you will probably have accumulated loads of back-up material while preparing your speech — dump it, because you won't be using it while you are on your feet.

The advantage of using one piece of card is that even if you drop it the 'pages' simply can't get out of order, and the discipline of making the bullets for a speech fit onto no more than four columns won't do you any harm either. For longer addresses an A4 sheet or card can be folded to provide six columns for your bullets — experiment with a spare sheet to establish in what order the columns should be written to keep the number of times you need to fold the card to a minimum while speaking.

A few final points on memory aids:

☐ If you are speaking at a lectern ensure that your notes (in whatever form) are not so low down that you bury your chin in your chest as you speak; apart from asphyxiating you it will destroy any eye contact with your victims. Tape, say, a piece of wood into place to hold your

binder or notes at the right level but check that the light is still effective.
- ☐ Check that a binder will actually open on the lectern without fouling the sides or microphone, or blocking out the light. Note where the switch is for the light.
- ☐ If the lectern is ultra hi-tech (some of them are like mission control units) *practise* with it beforehand. If you don't and you or your notes, or both, start rising up and down while you are speaking you will delight but distract your audience.
- ☐ Consider using a colour-coding system or pencilled brackets round points in your notes which can be deleted if you are not making any headway with your audience. Be sure you know which are the points you simply must make.
- ☐ Although you could put 'pause' points in your notes, use caution because if you rather obviously pause for laughter or applause and none comes then it can look a bit odd. Nothing says you can't plant a few 'applause leaders' in the audience, of course....
- ☐ I don't believe you should put gesture cues in your notes because the results may look artificial. In any case, however inexperienced you are as a speaker, I'm sure your natural instinct will make you turn to the chairman as you thank him for bringing the company back from the brink of bankruptcy. Don't worry too much about any spontaneous gestures you may make while speaking, although get a reliable friend to tip you off if, say, your arm waving simply becomes too distracting.

CHECKLIST 6

- ☐ Type text to be said, not read, e.g. 'it's' not 'it is'.
- ☐ Double spacing, upper and lower case.
- ☐ Watch page turnover points.
- ☐ Check that rings don't snag in a binder.
- ☐ Practise if using a cueing system. And have a full text nearby as a safeguard.
- ☐ Don't try to memorize your words.
- ☐ Bullet points may make you sound more spontaneous.
- ☐ Whatever system of notes you have, use fairly firm paper.
- ☐ Don't bow your head too much at a lectern.
- ☐ Use whatever system suits *you*.

7
VISUAL AIDS

I'm not sure if a picture is quite worth a thousand words but there is no doubt that visual aids can enhance a presentation and, by letting people see as well as hear information, help to put a message across. Nevertheless, before preparing *any* visual aids, ask yourself first if you can do without such support: will your presentation stand up on its own? If you conclude that you do need visuals (which, incidentally, would usually be out of place with after-dinner speeches) then first consider just how elaborate they should be. Major company presentations may feature drum and pipe bands, lasers and mounted cavalry (at least, it sometimes seems like that), but do watch that the fire and thunder approach does not fog the message you are trying to project; if people remember the TV star who appeared on stage with the managing director or can describe in detail your computerized slide show but can't recall the name of your new product, then you have failed.

The growth of computer-generated graphic slides for business presentations means that complicated slides can now be prepared very rapidly and, with computers also used to trigger multi-projectors, highly sophisticated presentations can result. However, if you are told in the days leading up to a presentation that you won't be able to react to circumstances and change a slide 'because it's in the computer', ease yourself out of the grip of technology next time and consider a simpler system. You want people to remember your message, not the hi-tech methods used to put it across. And remember that hi-tech can sometimes equal 'hi-risk'. Perfectionists will call for twin projectors for even a simple slide presentation (to avoid the slight gap between illustrations) but even something as harmless as that can lead to confusion if the slides are not fed into the carousels properly. Can't happen? Don't you believe it — I attended a presentation on slide techniques by an 'expert' recently...and the slides got out of order. Slides do get back to front and upside down. I am *not* suggesting you should eschew such support but it is no bad thing to have a healthy scepticism about technology.

And do watch the 'escalation factor' — the tendency for one company, or even one department within a company, to want to outdo another; the 'they went to Margate, we'd better go to Malta' syndrome. And consider: if you go over the top in your presentation you may irritate some of your audience, and they are liable to be the brightest and best. And no retailer of your range is likely to be impressed by an obviously expensive launch for a new product if he is seething because you have just pared down his discount.

So, be cautious about dancers and music accompanying a highly theatrical product announcement. If you do decide to take this route, then do get professional advice, because the timing must be perfect and guests, especially those who perhaps attend presentations by your competitors, will not be impressed by an amateurish affair. You are moving onto the fringes of show business — you need professionals to assist you. If in doubt, keep things short so that you reduce the likelihood of boredom; and do accept, by the way, that if you have a stirring song specially written about your company or product, then a parody is likely to be circulating within hours.

A QUESTION OF BALANCE

Despite these notes of caution, razzmatazz may still have a part to play — if you are presenting a new product to your sales team, or to customers, you certainly need to create an atmosphere that will enthuse people. As with so many business decisions, it is a question of balance. The judgement will obviously be influenced by the subject matter because an elaborate musical score and lavish light show would be inappropriate for many companies and their products. Similarly, tailor the lavishness of your visual aids to your audience and to the impression you hope to make on them. You might, for instance, decide to be less lavish with an internal than an external presentation. To some extent your approach to a presentation may be influenced by the numbers involved (if the numbers are large then a lavish approach may become cost-effective) as well as the 'richness' of your particular industry and the customs and practices within it; the motor industry, for instance, is renowned for the lavishness of its product launches.

Mind, you don't have to join the razzmatazz rat race and there is a case for varying things if you make regular presentations: put on an expensive show one year but consider a businesslike approach the next, perhaps with the money spent on a leading world figure to talk to the audience after lunch rather than on a military band. But, whether you take an elaborate or low-key approach, you should make an effort to be professional in whatever you do. The way you put your message across says something about your organization; if the slides are upside down or a projector fails, then it reflects adversely on your company.

Even at less elaborate functions, people will still remember more if they see as well as hear your presentation, while paying attention to simple details like dimming the lights to show visuals will create intimacy and add excitement even though you may then have less eye contact with your audience. But don't use visual aids as crutches to support poor presentations; write the words or draft the message first and then prepare visual aids. And remember that a poor visual aid will probably be worse than none at all because your audience will 'switch off' to your words as they struggle to comprehend the illustration. Your approach to visual aids should be as businesslike as it is to the words.

Bear in mind that visual aids can be expensive — very. So be certain you have the right information or illustration available, and check it carefully with the words *before* you commission anyone to prepare a slide or other aid. Work with rough outlines of the proposed visuals until you have settled the words; even if you are a bold ad-libber the need for visual aids should, happily, force you to give at least some thought to the structure of what you are going to say. And then do consider the question of confidentiality if you are having sensitive material made into visuals by outside companies.

You should use visuals to supplement rather than duplicate what you are saying. If you announce that you are sending top salesmen to Trinidad as a sales incentive prize and a visual comes up of an island,

I think you can assume that most will guess where it is. However, with something like a set of figures, you should refer to the information on show and not just leave it standing all forlorn.

Always err on the large side when having visuals prepared and don't put important information at the bottom of a flipchart or slide because, however hard you try, there may still be some people in the room who will not have a clear view. In fact, when did you last attend a function where everyone could see everything? Probably never.

Visual aids must be honest and if, for instance, you are showing a sales graph, don't make it steeper than it should be because you will lose credibility with the ones who notice your deceit. Unless total accuracy is needed, say for price increases or pay negotiations, use round figures. It will be easier to absorb 900 on a screen than 898 or 902. You should be consistent in presenting facts: if you show a percentage for one statistic, don't put '6 out of 10' for the next; and you should also be consistent in your selection of typefaces for visuals because if you keep swopping from one sort to another you will distract people: a uniform style will look more professional. If a series of speakers are to make presentations, efforts should be made to keep the same style among all their visual aids. It follows that, ideally, you should allow plenty of time to put a presentation together but if you commission visuals too far ahead you may end up having to redo some of them or, worse, show ones which are just slightly stale. It helps to have a good working relationship with the company preparing the visuals; pick one which is not afraid of midnight oil.

Colour can help to make visuals more interesting and easier to understand; for example, different colours can be used to indicate various stages of a sales chain or manufacturing process, thus simplifying otherwise complicated visuals. If several figures appear on a visual, and one is central to your theme, then circle or highlight it with a colour. Again, to assist comprehension, print any words horizontally rather than vertically on visual aids, even those on pie charts.

If you plan to use an illustration more than once, duplicate it rather than try to shuffle back to find it again during your presentation (which will look clumsy) while if you have a key visual, such as a video, it may be worth duplicating it in case the original copy is mislaid; it will help your peace of mind if nothing else. And if you are addressing foreigners, consider having visuals prepared in their language too — it will aid their comprehension, especially if you haven't got an interpreter. You could, for instance, consider a split screen with a slide in English on the left and a second language on the right.

Although some designers seem to love them, I think humorous drawings should be used with care; not everyone likes twee or supposedly funny cartoon characters. Cartoons should rarely be used for serious subjects. And, talking of serious subjects, do forewarn your audience if any gory visuals are to be shown, perhaps to illustrate a first aid lecture. If you have to break off to demonstrate resuscitation skills during your presentation, it will tend to disturb your flow.

It may be a nice touch to introduce speakers with a slide showing their photograph, name and title. Such photographs should be recent, not glamour shots taken years ago when they still had hair. Or, by way of light relief, they could be pictures of them taken when children.

Remember the mechanics involved with visual aids. Check that there will be such things as chalk, drawing pins, hammers, leads that are long enough for any electrical equipment, spare bulbs and something to stand projectors on (that last point was written with feeling because I've just given a lecture where I had to stand the projector on a crisp box wedged on a beer crate — it was an engineering society, incidentally). It's worth trying to get the quietest possible projection equipment because even the slight change of sound as a slide projector is switched off and then cools down at the end of a talk can be a mild distraction.

If you feel most comfortable with a particular form of visual aid, then use it. Don't mix visual aids too much; a little variety may be fine but if you switch from flipcharts to slides to video and back to flipcharts, the audience may become bewildered and certainly your projectionist will be quietly moaning.

But let us move on to consider a few specific types of visual aids. The simplest of all, of course, is to use your sparkling personality and this may be enough for one-to-one meetings or very small groups if you are properly briefed and have the relevant back-up material — brochures and so on.

An *actual object* to pass among an audience may make an effective visual aid and touching and holding something will be more powerful than any picture. But caution: the whispering and shuffling as an object gets passed around an audience will distract people. Better to tell them they can examine it at the end of your talk.

For small groups a *portable presentation case* may be useful. There are various sorts available; some fold out like small easels, others are housed within a briefcase (which makes them easy to carry around), but the basic principle is the same — they hold a series of clear plastic 'envelopes' into which you put cards, photographs, etc. The wallets are held on rings and you simply flip them over when you wish to move to the next visual. If your visuals are on stiffish card you may not need to use the plastic wallets; simply punch holes in the actual material. You should practise with whatever type you use to ensure that you can set it up quickly; a listener will not be impressed if your briefcase slides across the table and knocks over his coffee as you are telling him about your new wonder product.

Still with relatively small groups, *computers* may have a role to play. People are usually naive enough to trust computers implicitly and you may make a good impression with a microcomputer that is programmed to give an immediate answer to customers' problems when they have given you one or two pieces of information. A printer will also leave them with a copy of your conclusion. The same equipment can feed back information to your office or stores via phone; keep track of sales calls; retain details of a client's order, etc. It will even keep a record of your expenses, although you may have your own reasons for not wanting it to do this. A computer is worth considering *only* if you learn how to use it properly; if you do, you will be conveying to people that yours is an alert, progressive company. Mind, you must remember the purpose of your presentation — don't concentrate on the wonders of the computer so much that you leave customers more concerned about acquiring one themselves than buying the product you originally called to sell them.

The humble *blackboard* is cheap and simple, and

can be quite suitable when presenting to largish groups where an ultra-professional approach is not needed. Ensure that the easel is stable with the pegs taped in place at the right height. More attractive are *magnetic boards* where you have magnetic pieces representing various products or processes which you stick on the board during your presentation. Or you could use a *white board* on which you write with special coloured markers. Such boards are available double-sided so that you can swing a clean face into play when the first is full. If your budget will stretch even further, you can obtain boards with built-in *photocopies* so that you can hand round A4 copies of what you have written. If you alert delegates to this facility it will mean that they can concentrate on your presentation without having to take notes.

Simpler and cheaper are *flipcharts*. As the name suggests, flipcharts are really just larger versions of the portable presentation cases; they are illustrations, either on card or paper, mounted on freestanding or table-top easels and flipped over (or aside) as you move through your presentation. The charts can either be ledged on an easel or held together by rings at the top ready to be flipped over. By having plain sheets as well as prepared illustrations available it is possible to move from a set presentation to a more informal session during which you jot figures or whatever down before your listeners' very eyes. You may in such cases find feint ruled sheets most convenient to give a neat result. If you make regular presentations on a particular subject you could have flipcharts with most of the material ready printed on washable sheets with gaps in which you write facts or figures as you make your pitch. You could have a line saying 'Sales last year' followed by a gap, then ask the audience to guess what the sales were before writing in the actual figure. Remember to wipe it off before your next performance.

If you plan to draw on a flipchart during your presentation, cheat a little by lightly pencilling in an outline beforehand. You will then be able to draw over the lines with a felt tip or whatever with a great air of confidence. (You can use the same trick with thin chalk marks on a blackboard.)

Many regular presenters have a soft spot for flipcharts because they are simple to work and don't entail any fiddling with power supplies or lighting. However, charts must be kept clean and up to date; house them in a suitable carrying-case or at least select a size that will go under your arm, otherwise they can be awkward and tiring to carry about.

Proper use of an *overhead projector* can give a relaxed flavour to a presentation because the speaker faces the audience and the transparent sheets can be drawn in their entirety or modified during an actual meeting — you can circle figures or underline words as you go along. Make use of colour but remember that a typewriter face may not be large enough to read from the back of a large room. For a detailed presentation you can overlay one image on top of another to build up a story, although for elaborate illustrations it is probably better to prepare separate transparencies for each stage. A small point: separate the transparencies from their protective paper sheets *before* your presentation otherwise, if you fumble when doing so, it may mar the flow.

It is possible to obtain OHPs with attachments which allow a continuous roll of clear acetate to be used if you are planning to draw a lot of illustrations as you talk. If you have ready-prepared transparencies it is worth mounting them in card frames to protect them. Incidentally, an important advantage with an OHP is that you don't have to switch the lights off. Equally useful may be the fact that it is possible to run off duplicate sets of transparencies for an OHP simply by feeding the acetate sheets through a photocopier.

If you wish to show an audience such things as press cuttings and photographs without the trouble of making slides of them, then use an *episcope*, but bear in mind that you will need to put the lights off when doing so.

Although overworked, *slides* are still among the most effective visual aids. They can be produced both quickly and relatively cheaply, but they still cost money, so keep in mind the earlier advice to get your words right first. If you are tempted to use multi-projectors and slides which vibrate or otherwise amaze with their versatility, why not consider video instead? If you do use slides, bear in mind the following:

☐ Keep to a maximum of 15 to 20 words and 25 to 30 numbers per slide, otherwise they will become confusing. And leave space between the lines if you are having slides prepared from typescript or this too will make them difficult to read.

☐ 'Build-up' slides of such things as sales figures (which reveal first one piece of information then two and so on) are an effective way of putting information across, but such slides must be carefully made and put in special registration mounts, otherwise a slight jump between one slide and the next will distract. If you have such

a series of slides made, consider using a different colour for the new piece of information shown each time. As an alternative to 'build-up' slides, you could have a split screen effect where two or more illustrations appear at the same time.
- [ ] A carousel holds 80 slides, so try not to end up with 81 or, if making a marathon presentation, 161 or so.
- [ ] If you do a lot of presentations with slides, a light box (an opaque flat surface with a variable light underneath) will be helpful because you can lay your slides on it to select and sort them. And when you've done so, don't forget to clean the slides — the slightest mark or speck of dust will show only too clearly on a screen.
- [ ] Be ruthless in excluding holiday slides from a presentation (they have been known to slip in) unless you have just one jokey shot of the audience when they were away on an incentive trip together.
- [ ] Avoid 'good morning' or any other word slides which really add nothing to a meeting; put a symbol or logo on the screen if there is an unavoidable pause between other illustrations.
- [ ] Use plastic mounts for slides rather than cardboard ones, which can sometimes buckle.
- [ ] Make quite sure you know how to use the remote control for a projector before a presentation starts. If you fiddle with the control, perhaps through nerves, you may inadvertently reveal the slide containing your key message before you have built up to it in your speech.
- [ ] Put a blank slide at the start of a series so that you can switch on the projector to check if it is working without anything showing on the

screen. And remember to put blanks in the carousel at any point when you will be showing film or video.
- ☐ Have a few blank or bland 'wallpaper' slides available so that you can, for example, insert one if you have to withdraw a slide at the last moment because it has become obsolete.

Mark slide change points very clearly in your script (some speakers have one page of script per slide but this can become cumbersome) and give the projectionist a duplicate if you are not working the equipment yourself. Allow for the brief time the projector will take to work and either circle the word on which you want the slide to change, like this:

'...now let us turn (to) exports...'

or put a mark at that point, e.g.

'...moving on to the ∧ northern district...'

or, perhaps best of all, break your script around the slides like this:

'...I would now like to talk about
SLIDE 7 — SALES TARGETS
our sales targets for the next three months'.

You or the projectionist would have to be asleep to miss such a change point and you will quickly get used to ignoring the slide words as you read your script. Whatever system you use, and it doesn't matter what it is provided you are comfortable with it, you may find it helpful to have an illustration of every slide either in among your text or on the facing page so that you know exactly what is on the screen without having to keep looking at it. If you add further back-up information on the facing page you will be well armed if you take questions later.

You may wish to use a *film* during your presentation but, if so, be sure that there is someone who understands the equipment. If you have several films or sections of film to show, consider joining them together with blank or plain-coloured lengths of film so that it is possible to leave the projector running once you start. Time the blank linking pieces and then write and carefully rehearse words to fit them. Make sure the microphone is live for such linking peices and don't make them so long that your timing goes awry. Let me stress that you should rehearse the sections between linked films so that you deliver the words with confidence rather than rushing to be sure of finishing them before the next clip begins.

An elaborate slide-tape presentation which is to be shown several times could be put onto *video* and there will often be other uses for video too. This is an area that has expanded rapidly and will continue to do so for a while yet. With interactive video disc systems it is possible for training or sales purposes, and at exhibitions, to conduct a two-way exchange with answers to questions determining what is next shown on a screen (eventually people will buy from video and holographic displays and we will all become redundant). If you think this is too complicated to use and won't become commonplace, just look at the queues in front of bank cash dispensers. If you have a clever process to demonstrate, a short video will do so better than any brochure or spoken words. But video is expensive and there are a lot of people willing to convince you that you want art for art's sake, so go into video with a level head. Consider some other uses for the videos you make; perhaps they can be shown to local groups as part of a community relations programme.

If you feel there may be a foreign application for

a video or film you commission (don't laugh — communication frontiers are breaking down), avoid having too many people talking English to camera and don't fit the commentary too tightly to the pictures because commentaries in more long-winded languages will need more time.

By the way, it may be worth starting any film or video with a section of music or other attention-grabbing sound; don't plunge straight into the commentary because there may be times when an audience will be chattering or still filtering in when a show starts.

Incidentally, at large venues you may find yourself projected onto a screen as you speak via a video system so that people at the back can see you. If so, do guard against any distressing personal habits which might otherwise go unnoticed.

One final point about videos, and film, for that matter: don't try to reach too many different audiences with one production or you will end up with something too bland to enthuse any of your targets. But do remember that people will have been conditioned to professional standards by watching TV (well, some of it, anyway) so don't let your production look amateurish. Don't let your projection of video look amateurish either — have an experienced operator if possible so that you avoid the few seconds pause (which seem an eternity) when a video is to start.

This is by no means an exhaustive list of visual aids — there are filmstrips, loop films, models (live and scale) and so on — but it is probably enough to be going on with. Remember when using many visual aids that you will need a clean screen, which should be stable and mounted as high as possible for good visibility. Consider back projection (i.e.

with the equipment behind the screen) if space in the audience area is limited; this will look slightly more professional too because there will be no light beaming through the audience and no shadow heads will appear as latecomers move to their seats; furthermore you will not have the disruption to the seating caused by a projector standing in the middle.

One important point — having considered what visuals to put *on*, give equal thought to when to take them *off*. It is distracting and ultimately mildly irritating to leave a chart or picture on display long after you have finished talking about it. Far better to move to a blank screen or one with a logo, conference title or wallpaper on instead.

Incidentally, however carefully you have planned your visual aids, there may still be times when you need to point to a particular point to emphasize it. Pointers which retract to the size of a ballpen are convenient to carry around, snooker cues or canes may suffice, while battery powered units which throw a light marker onto a screen are effective provided you learn to control them properly. Your choice.

As a footnote, consider whether a post-presentation visual aid may be appropriate, such as one or more sheets summarizing the key points, with illustrations of the visuals used; if you are talking about your company to an outside group why not have brochures available for guests to take away? The degree of hard sell you indulge in on such occasions will have to be left to your natural tact and charm.

It is not worth putting a special heading in the book for it, but an *audio* aid may be appropriate on occasions. If you are trying to encourage staff to handle incoming phone calls better, a recording of a few awful instances could be entirely appropriate as well as highly effective. But ensure that you know how the recorder works and do avoid any long pauses after you have introduced something, as mentioned with video, a pause doesn't have to be very long to seem like an eternity.

LIGHTING

Perhaps one of the most useful but neglected forms of visual aid is lighting, which can be used very effectively to control or change the 'mood' of a room. The level of lighting needed will vary according to what, if any, visual aids you are using, because for films and slides (as well as videos projected onto a large screen) it will help if at least the lights immediately above the screen can be switched off.

Here are a few other points to keep in mind about lighting:

- ☐ The organizer should ask someone to be in sole charge and to find out where switches are and which lights they operate. Remove a few bulbs if this is the only way to balance the lighting to your liking. If you are presenting in a strange venue then take the trouble to sort things out with your hosts beforehand.
- ☐ There must be a light on a lectern and it should be securely fixed so that it does not get in the way of scripts or binders.
- ☐ Even if someone is just saying a few words at a cocktail party or coffee gathering, they should stand where the light is brightest and on a stool or table so that they can be clearly seen — a disembodied voice is confusing.

- Presenters should be lit but not blinded.
- Lights can be used to 'control' an audience to some extent. If the lights dim it will be seen as a signal that things are about to start.
- Don't turn the lights on and off too often during a presentation because this is distracting. Remember that if you leave the lights off too long after lunch some of the audience will go to sleep.
- If possible, put roving spotlights onto speakers or, for example, prizewinners as they move to the front. After a presentation, speakers should have enough light to see as they leave a stage so that they do not trip over a step as their eyes readjust.
- Some conferences have 'traffic lights' on lecterns so that a chairperson can signal when a speaker has, say, a minute left and when they must stop. I hope your presentation will have slightly more flexibility about it, although all presenters should avoid overstaying their welcome.
- *Electricity can be dangerous.* Obvious, of course, but don't take chances. Don't let amateurs fiddle with equipment. Do tape down any wires that may be trailing about the place to stop people tripping over them. We don't want to lose you. Having said that, I should perhaps add that doing away with electricity altogether can be effective — at least one of the colleges in Cambridge has a dining room with no electricity, just candles for illumination. Delightful for an elegant business dinner but presenting a different set of problems, like how to read your notes and how to avoid them catching fire!

CHECKLIST 7

☐ Can you do without visual aids?

☐ Prepare words *before* visuals.

☐ Don't get trapped by the technology.

☐ Use visuals to supplement, rather than duplicate, the words.

☐ Err on the large side for words and illustrations.

☐ Visual aids must be honest.

☐ Be consistent in your methods when presenting facts.

☐ Use colours to highlight key points or show different processes.

☐ Be wary with humorous drawings.

☐ Check the mechanics — long leads, plugs, pins, etc.

☐ Be wary of passing objects around an audience. Wait until after your pitch.

☐ Practise with your visual aids system; liaise with any projectionist; mark change points clearly in your text.

☐ Avoid bobbing about from one visual aid system to another.

- [ ] Be professional in what you do — people are conditioned to high standards on TV, etc.

- [ ] Check who will be working the lights.

- [ ] Remember that electricity can be dangerous. Take care!

- [ ] Use whatever visual aids make you feel comfortable.

8
REHEARSALS

Having given careful thought to your audience and devised what you are going to say to them, it makes sense to complete your preparation process by rehearsing your speech or presentation. The degree of effort you should put into this depends to a large extent on the meeting concerned. If you are involved in a full-scale business presentation with lavish visuals, celebrities, racing camels and whatever then there must be at least one full dress rehearsal — in fact, there will probably be at least two, of which the first will simply by a 'stagger through' to check that the visuals are in the right order and so on. Ideally, rehearsals should take place in the actual venue and they should highlight and help eradicate any problems, for instance speakers bumping into each other as they change over. If presenters have a long walk to a podium they should start moving up as they are being introduced to avoid uneasy pauses; they should try to arrive with apparent confidence no matter how nervous they may be.

Rehearsals should help to establish the right lighting levels and they should provide an opportunity to sort out any public address systems. *Everyone* involved in a presentation should be included in the rehearsal(s) because if not, a managing director, scheduled to say just a few words of welcome, may then nonchalantly add '...and I know you are going to be delighted that we've cut the price by 25 per cent' when that was supposed to come 45 minutes later as the highlight of the conference following a laser show and a rather moving ballet sequence by the Roly Polys.

Incidentally, if a presentation is to be made to several audiences of different sizes, introduction sequences should be programmed accordingly. If your presentation starts with a computer-controlled sequence of slides and music to give people time to sit down, and this is prepared for a large audience, it may be too long for a smaller group and will keep churning away long after they have sat down, which will kill some of the anticipatory atmosphere. The answer will be to start the sequence and let it run for a while before calling people in. Check the timing carefully; it is even worth keeping a log of how long it takes an audience to move into your venue, how long it takes to serve them coffee and so on.

If you are a speaker involved in a major presentation then use a rehearsal to make yourself thoroughly familiar with how you are going to get on and off stage, and above all of course with your words. If your words have been written for you by someone else, be sure you are happy with the content and style, otherwise you will not be very convincing; remember to look up fairly frequently when rehearsing to get used to developing eye contact with your audience.

There is likely to be a build-up of tension as 'opening night' approaches — the theatrical comparison is entirely apt because to a large extent you are entering show business — but do not become neurotic about it all: it is a bit late to start fussing over a tiny and irrelevant detail on a slide. Conversely, however, if there is a major change needed (perhaps because of a significant news break affecting your business) then you may have to insist to the organizer that a change is made.

If you are making a less lavish but none the less important presentation to existing or potential *customers*, it may be important to 'rehearse' your knowledge of the product or service you are offering, because without a total command of your subject you will never convince anyone of its worth. If necessary organize a light-hearted inter-staff quiz to test knowledge of a new product, and take part yourself too.

Next, consider who will be attending the meeting, be clear on their level of importance and try to establish who is the key decision maker. If other areas of your company interface with the people you are presenting to, consult them to find out how relations stand and if any problems are likely to be raised. This research may alert you if, for instance, one of the customer's team is anxious to see your product bought because it helps his own work; he may be a useful ally at the presentation. If you know that one of your staff has a personality clash with one of your customer's people, perhaps a diplomatic cold could keep him away.

If you know your customers well, a phone call beforehand to explain what form you intend the presentation to take and to check if this suits them will help to prepare the ground; they will find it less easy to object if they have agreed an outline agenda in advance.

Clarify who is to speak about what and devise a few inter-company coded signals, e.g. if the boss puts his hand on top of his head it means that whoever is speaking should shut up smartly.

If you are rehearsing a solo *talk* or *lecture* then say it aloud or 'in your head' a few times so that you establish whether you are happy with the content and words. It may be appropriate to consider whether you have any high and low points in your presentation — you really need to have to avoid it becoming monotonous. And at the risk of becoming monotonous as an author, have you considered your audience? Is your talk geared to their needs, expectations, level of intelligence and interest in your subject? It should be. Make sure you familiarize yourself with any visual aids during a rehearsal — if you find that you fumble when flicking over a particular chart then modify your system so that things run smoothly on the day.

Perhaps the most difficult thing to rehearse is a *speech* during which you hope to motivate or entertain. Difficult because without an audience it is, for instance, almost impossible to sense how jokes will be received. All you can do is say the words to yourself a time or two so that you become familiar with the links between one section and the next; you will have less problem with a more formal speech which is to be read. With either case, tape recording your rehearsal, while by no means essential, may at least alert you to any unsettling 'ers', 'you knows' and the like.

You need to strike a balance when rehearsing speeches — do enough to iron out any snags but don't do so much that you kill any freshness and sense of spontaneity.

If you have a major speech to make, such as to an influential trade association, and the success of it could enhance your career or company, then you may consider cribbing an idea from the theatre and practise your big speech in front of a less important audience somewhere. Television performers sometimes try out new material in small clubs before using it on the box, while shows tour the provinces as a shake-down before moving into the West End — if you do something similar it may at least alert you to which jokes to delete.

Irrespective of the proposed function, keep the following in mind about rehearsals:

☐ Try to establish a realistic idea of the running time. It is essential to have accurate timing for a major conference if a large number of people have to be fed; for less elaborate functions it still helps to have an idea of time. It may not be easy to get an accurate fix for a speech where there will be laughter (you hope) and applause, but you at least need to know if your speech will be 15 or 25 minutes. And do remember that, to my knowledge, no one has ever been savaged for being too brief; lots have for being too long-winded, so if in doubt, cut.

☐ Familiarize yourself with any equipment — for instance, if you are to operate a projector, sort out exactly how the thing works.

☐ Establish who is going to switch lights on and off — calling for this to be done during a presentation can seem a bit amateurish.

☐ Check that you can see your notes. If you are at a podium or lectern, is it at the right height for you to be seen? The height of many lecterns can be adjusted but, if not, get a box to stand on. Some regular after-dinner speakers even cart round their own portable lecterns to rest their notes on but, if you do the same, don't use one which is so elaborate that it needs planning permission, because the pantomime of erecting it may become too prolonged.

☐ Practise if you have to use a cueing system

because it may take a little while to get used to the rather short lines of text. Some old stagers actually look down occasionally when using such systems so that it looks as if they are reading from notes — in fact, that is when they are ad-libbing because they are not actually seeing anything. Such tricks are entirely harmless.

- [ ] Rehearse in the same position you will be in 'on the day'; if you are due to be standing up (which is preferable) then stand up when you rehearse. Don't try rehearsing in front of a mirror — unnatural and quite unnecessary.
- [ ] Ask a friend whose judgement you respect to sit in during your rehearsal to see if he or she can understand a word of what you are saying. Caution: if you are a boffin due to speak to a general audience, don't ask a fellow boffin to sit in because he will understand your rarified ramblings — use a layman as a guinea pig instead. If a series of presentations is to be made, someone should sit in on the rehearsals for all of them to warn against clashes or inconsistencies among the various speakers.
- [ ] Don't attempt to rehearse gestures; these should be spontaneous or not done at all. However, do ask your auditing friend mentioned above to alert you to any distressing mannerisms you may have (such as jangling coins in a pocket) which will be off-putting for an audience.
- [ ] Use rehearsals to rehearse 'applause leaders' if you feel you need them to start applause going. Don't wince, such sycophants are used at political rallies, so why not use them too to add sparkle to your desperately interesting review of the future prospects for pig iron or whatever

is currently turning you on? Don't overdo the applause but the odd ripple here and there (triggered by the one or two who have been briefed) won't do any harm.

- [ ] If you have a long speech or presentation to make (and you should first ask yourself *why*?) then rehearse at full cry otherwise you may find your voice fading when you perform for real. If you find this is a problem and you don't speak very often, consider reading books aloud to improve your stamina; you could even do it to the bedridden in a local hospital to get an audience reaction (at least they won't be able to walk out).

After you have completed your rehearsal, try to sit back and consider the *overall* effect. Would things be improved with a different running order? Have you held on to your message? Do the words and any visual aids harmonize or are there slides on the screen long after you have finished referring to them? Do you readily get your tongue round your words? If not, modify them. Are you comfortable with the memory aids you plan to use? If not, change the system. Is the length about right?

Invariably, 'panic stations' becomes the norm as a major presentation looms, with people so busy settling items of detail that no one finds time to take a calm overview. Try not to fall into the same trap yourself, whether you are part of a major conference or just giving a talk to a few people. As a business discipline it is even worth taking out the objectives you were advised to write down all these chapters ago. Is your address going to meet them? Better to make one final effort to ensure that it does rather than be left with an unsatisfactory feeling after the big day.

Like so much in business, rehearsing is a question of balance — a balance between doing too little and having lights on at the wrong time or slides upside down, or doing too much and making it all a shade glib, delivered in a very self-satisfied voice (whatever you do don't make it too obvious that you like the sound of it).

CHECKLIST 8

- ☐ Do a full 'stagger through' as well as a dress rehearsal if it is a lavish presentation.

- ☐ Note how to get on and off stage.

- ☐ Rehearse speeches enough to be familiar but not so much as to become stale.

- ☐ Say your words aloud to get your tongue round them.

- ☐ Tape recording your rehearsal is not essential.

- ☐ Rehearsing in front of a mirror is not recommended.

- ☐ Get a friend to sit in on rehearsals and play devil's advocate.

- ☐ Use rehearsals to sort out public address system, visual aids, lighting, etc.

- ☐ Can you see your notes? Will the audience be able to see you?

- ☐ Re-jig your speech if it still doesn't flow properly.

- ☐ Watch the length. If in doubt, cut.

- ☐ If presenting to potential customers, rehearse your knowledge of your product.

- ☐ Develop inter-company signals, e.g. when to shut up.

9
GETTING ON WITH YOUR NERVES

Grown men and women who cheerfully face danger when skiing, mountaineering or motor racing become afraid when faced with the task of speaking in public. If you analyse it, this is quite absurd because no one ever gets physically hurt when speaking. Well, hardly ever — the exceptions may be politicians who occasionally get things thrown at them but we need not be overly bothered about their welfare.

It must be the psychological battering that we all fear, the fear of failing. (I say 'all' — if you are firmly convinced that you are the exception and are not troubled by nerves, well, are you sure you are not just a shade complacent or, worse, even arrogant and not thinking enough of your audiences?) If you are slightly nervous, even at the thought of reading a presentation to a group of colleagues you meet every day, then take comfort from the fact that you are not alone. Surveys show that among many people the fear of speaking is greater than that of flying, spiders or having your key to the executive washroom withdrawn, and fear certainly leads many people to refuse opportunities to speak.

The first step in getting your nerves under control may be to accept the fact that you may never be able to conquer them entirely; in fact, total control of nerves may be undesirable because a certain amount of nervousness can add sparkle to a presentation or speech by making you more alert. Nervous tension is a perfectly normal reaction with any strong emotion and is something of a throwback to uncivilized life thousands of years ago (slightly less at some rumbustious sales meetings) when meeting an opponent meant that you had to put the maximum effort into either fighting or running away. The emotion starts adrenalin chasing about your body, your heart rate increases, your blood pressure rises and sweat glands in the skin work overtime to carry away the excess heat produced, which explains the sweaty palms and the endless trips to the lavatory. It's not just public speakers who are affected. Ronnie Barker mentions in his book *It's hello from him!* that he was as nervous at first nights and recordings at the end of his career as he was as a teenager, and notice how athletes fiddle with necklaces before they run — even wearing them as a talisman may be a form of nerves because logic suggests that anything that adds extra weight to a runner must be wrong.

WHY ARE YOU NERVOUS?

It may be worth considering if there are specific reasons for your nerves, other than the general tension most people have. Are you nervous because of inexperience? Well, if so, you have really got to start sometime (perhaps by joining a speakers club or debating society) because it's virtually impossible to live a business life without speaking; if you remain silent you will seem gormless or it will be assumed that you have joined some strange and silent religious sect. Frankly, neither conclusion will do your career a lot of good. Conversely, speaking well could enhance your career — if nothing else you should be able to perform better at job interviews.

If you are nervous because you are not too familiar with the subject then either refuse to speak or, if you simply have to (perhaps as the managing director at a conference of specialists), then get your words checked by a knowledgeable colleague and structure the meeting so that your own lack of detailed knowledge is not exposed. On no account take questions.

If you are nervous at the thought of proposing a toast or vote of thanks at a formal business association dinner that sounds a bit grand, then don't be frightened because these are probably the easiest occasions on which to speak. A vote of thanks simply means that you are acting as a spokesman for the rest of the audience in saying 'thank you' to someone; the biggest snag is that you at least will have to stay awake and pay some attention to what a boring speaker (and, ye gods, they can be boring at professional dinners) is saying. A toast can be equally simple and may only entail digging out a few relevant facts for your preamble — such as isn't it jolly good that membership has doubled.

But even assuming that nerves are perfectly natural, can any steps be taken to get them loosely under control? Try these:

1 Get as much practise as possible and seize any opportunity to speak. There are countless social groups searching for speakers and unless your business is desperately dull you should find willing victims. In fact, even if your business *is* boring, you could try speaking on a more general topic such as 'Business in the next

century' or whatever. And why not read the lesson at your local church to get experience in addressing an audience?
2 As suggested in the chapter on rehearsing, try reading aloud either to yourself or friends; if nothing else this will strengthen your voice but it may also make you more confident.
3 Know your subject. Confidence in your knowledge will help you to relax and control your nerves, but don't relax so much that you send your audience to sleep — a point that boffins or the very knowledgeable need to watch when addressing less erudite audiences. If you make sludge dispersal pumps don't, please don't, describe the valves in detail when you speak at a local Women's Institute. And I think I'd save some of the subtleties of sewage disposal until after the coffee too.
4 Recognize that the subject on which you are speaking may affect your nervous tension, because if you are raising an unpopular topic you may anticipate that the going will get rough; telling a bunch of retailers that their margins are to be cut is never easy.
5 If you are attending a function where you feel there is even a remote chance that you will be asked to say a few words, then give a little thought to what you might say. Having said that, I don't always follow my own advice. When I attended the dinner at which the Benedictine After-Dinner Speakers Awards were presented (you didn't expect me to go through the book without immodestly mentioning them, did you?) I was so convinced that I was just there to make up the numbers that I didn't prepare anything...and was therefore thrown when

asked to say a few words at five minutes' notice, and did a less effective job as a result. So, if you are attending anything where you might be speaking, prepare a little to avoid being tongue-tied on the day. Obviously, if you feel you may be one of a handful of people in line for a particular award, you should not prepare a detailed 10-minute address, nor should you produce a sheaf of notes if you receive an award, but there is no harm in idly considering what you might say, who you should thank and so on, if you are a winner. It's not arrogance, just self-preservation.

6   Don't worry if you stutter. I've heard people with speech impediments give brilliant addresses, partly because they had the glorious confidence to make the handicap work in their favour.

7   Don't, please don't, try to steady your nerves with drugs or drink. The effects of the former may be unpredictable, while the influence of the latter may be all too obvious as you stumble or slur your words (and a microphone will cruelly magnify this). Some people believe one glass of wine relaxes them but a problem, particularly at dinners, is that over-attentive waiters may keep topping you up without your noticing so that you take more than one glass. Take two and you may be in trouble, especially if you do a radio or TV interview after a speech, as sometimes happens. Driving home afterwards may present its own hazards too.

Should business people go on courses to learn public speaking and help steady their nerves? On balance probably 'yes', although choose a course with care — word of mouth is the best route — and monitor the effect (if any) on the first guinea pig from a company to go before sending others.

If I have any reservations about such courses it is that they seem to produce a 'sameness' among business speakers; if you study the executive in public, charisma isn't exactly the first word that springs to mind, is it? Nevertheless, a training course should improve your confidence and competence; if nothing else it may indicate who in a company should positively *not* be the public spokesperson if disaster ever strikes.

Now that many companies have their own video equipment (perhaps used for other training purposes) it may be cheaper and maybe no less effective to experiment with in-house training courses. Several videos are available that illustrate the key points to keep in mind about speaking and, after watching one, individuals could be asked to stand up and give a brief speech to the rest of the group on a subject they have prepared beforehand. If these speeches are filmed and played back on a TV screen while the group is encouraged by the trainer to be mercilessly critical of one another, the results can be remarkably beneficial (and revealing). After their prepared speeches participants could be asked to ad lib for a minute or so on a subject pulled out of a hat. Having to speak off the cuff on, say, 'Why we should use the local Little Chef rather than Le Manoir aux Quat' Saisons to reduce business overheads' will give students so much to think about that they will forget their nerves. The atmosphere of gentle ribaldry that can develop on such in-house occasions can actually help relax nerves, and the outline described — which can be modified with experience — is not too dissimilar from some of the professional training courses on offer.

But enough. If you have analysed your audience, if you know your subject and have prepared your words carefully and if you have done sufficient rehearsing, then you have done all you can. Relax (or try to), with just one caveat: if it all goes well, don't get too relaxed afterwards if there are journalists present — your relief may make you indiscreet.

CHECKLIST 9

☐ Almost everyone suffers from nerves. If you don't, maybe you aren't taking things seriously enough.

☐ Being nervous may make you perform better.

☐ Nerves can be controlled if not conquered.

☐ Practise speaking. Seize any opportunity.

☐ Consider public speaking courses. Simple in-house ones can be effective.

☐ Know what you are talking about.

☐ Don't use drugs or drink to steady your nerves.

10
COUNTDOWN

Although your key preparation is done when you have prepared and rehearsed your words, there are other things you can do as a speech or presentation approaches in order to help make it a success. For example: give yourself plenty of time to get to the venue — you won't be at your best if you arrive sweating and cursing at the last minute, having failed to find either the venue or somewhere to park. And are you looking your best? Is your hair fairly tidy and are you properly dressed for the occasion? For purely business functions, a traditional business suit will probably be the correct wear for men, although ideally it should not be too dark or sombre. Women have much more choice, of course, but perhaps should not wear anything too flamboyant. On other occasions take the trouble to find out what the rest will be wearing — for instance, if it says 'dress optional' on a ticket ask the organizer if the top table at least will be in evening dress. If in doubt, at dinners it is probably better to be slightly overdressed, rather than underdressed (even if someone does mistake you for a waiter and asks for the cigars) because, as a speaker, you will be on display.

For less formal occasions, 'smart casual wear' may be appropriate. You as a speaker should be smartly turned out, without looking like a colour-coordinated member of the chorus line. I think chief executives need to take care when dropping in to make presentations to people who are in pullovers and flannels, such as on a training course; a slightly less formal business suit may be a happier compromise for men on such occasions. Give the same thought to dress if speaking to an outside organization on an informal occasion — you may look out of place in a village hall in waistcoat and spats, or smart skirt and jacket, if the audience is in anoraks, and this may erect a small barrier before you have even opened your mouth. Ask the organizer what people usually wear on such occasions.

I guess clothing is one area where women are at a mild disadvantage because their appearances are likely to be examined more critically than those of the men, who are able to shelter behind their anonymous suits. Anyway, if you are a woman making your way in business you will already have evolved your own dress code and you will not need any advice from me. I am sure you will know that wearing a brief mini skirt will attract attention, but not to your words, so you probably won't wear one; try to enthuse your audience with well-turned phrases rather than ankles. Both sexes should avoid wearing anything tight around the neck for obvious reasons and they should not wear jangling jewellery because it may distract or reflect any spotlights.

Take your script or notes with you when you leave for the venue and make a note of any points that need clarifying when you arrive, e.g. do you need to refer to an association or federation? Remember you may need money for cloakroom tips or raffles; many functions nowadays ask guests to put their names on £5 or £10 notes to raise funds for worthy causes. I know it's probably illegal to deface the currency but it happens and you'll look a bit mean trying to write on a pound coin with a ballpen if you haven't any notes with you. Incidentally, if you are taking guests to these functions you ought to alert them if such fund-raising occurs.

All the above happens before you get to the venue; you should take further steps in the build-up to your big moment when you arrive, for example:

- ☐ Go into the room where you will be speaking and stand at the designated spot. Will you be in the right place in relation to your audience? If there is a table plan for a dinner, note whether you are sitting between appropriate people. Ideally, if speaking to an outside group at a dinner, you need to be next to at least one person from the organization so that you can check topical references to help you fine tune your address.
- ☐ Will you need a microphone? Public address systems cause so many ulcers for speakers that they have the next chapter all to themselves.
- ☐ Is the podium, if used, at the right height for you? If not, can you modify it?
- ☐ Get the answers to any open points listed in your notes.
- ☐ Double check people's names if you are going to refer to them. If you call Mr Wilson, Watson, you won't deserve to clinch a sale. Don't be thrown off balance if, say, the chairman is unavoidably absent and the managing director has taken his place; just carefully go through your notes and make any appropriate alterations.
- ☐ Mention to the host if you plan to rib someone (gently) in your address — you will look an oaf if you joke about someone who has just had a misfortune or is absent.

- [ ] Check whether the press has been invited as this may affect how frank you wish to be. If, of course, you are present to put over a message and are actively seeking coverage then let journalists have a copy of your key section, and offer to do interviews for any radio and television people present.
- [ ] If your peroration is to be followed by a questions session, suggest one or two suitable ones to the host and ask him to get people to raise them to get things going.
- [ ] Introduce yourself to the toastmaster, chairperson or master of ceremonies and check how they plan to announce you. If, for instance, your job title helps to establish your right to be addressing the audience on a particular topic then ask for it to be announced after your name.
- [ ] If the host is to speak before you do, try to establish exactly what he is going to say about you — he may, for instance, be working from out-of-date biographical details, while his words may affect how the audience responds to you. If you are portrayed as something of a 'know-all' there may be mild hostility towards you; and even if you have a reputation as a fine or amusing speaker, I would try to persuade the chair not to make too much of this otherwise the audience may sit there thinking 'go on then, amuse me'. Discourage people from droning on about you; a few key points to establish why you are there should be enough. The safest guarantee of being introduced properly is to write out a few appropriate words about yourself for the chairperson to use. Gently hint that these words will be more effective if it is not stated openly that you have written them. Occasionally, you

will encounter a host who thinks it is smart to do an offensively (rather than humorously) jokey or even sarcastic introduction — either take a verbal swipe at such people in your speech or, preferably, ignore the rudeness.

☐ Establish exactly what else will be happening besides your performance, and if the organizer has a typed timetable ask to see it because that way you will find out in advance that your speech is to be preceded by a raffle or charity auction or even (and it has happened to me) a long presentation on a cause that guests are being asked to support — such causes may be worthy but if the audience is dabbing away its tears at the plight of others as you start, its members may need time to adjust to your perhaps more robust message.

I am not suggesting that you should become a pain in the neck and make an organizer's life a misery by trying to change things, but if you are the one who has to stand up then a little thought to these points is not out of place. If you say tactfully, 'The last time I spoke with the podium in a corner like that such-and-such happened...', then a switched-on organizer will take the hint and rearrange the position. Talking of podiums, I was going to suggest that for after-dinner speeches it is better to stay at your table rather than move to a podium, but now I'm not so sure because I've just spoken at the Meridien in Piccadilly and their layout of the speaking area with a podium on a stage in a small alcove is well-nigh perfect. At least you will be seen by everyone if you move onto some sort of raised area; your choice. By the way, if you are to speak away from where you will be sitting, check how

you will get on and off stage.
- ☐ Find out what is to happen at the end of your pitch. Are you to propose a toast, take questions, hand over to a chairperson, introduce the next speaker or...? Better to find out beforehand than flounder at the finish.
- ☐ Check whether a supply of water will be available where you are speaking as nerves may give you a dry throat. Don't have the water too iced as this may make the problem worse.

Most of the above assumes that you are speaking at your own or a 'neutral' venue. Sometimes, of course, when making a presentation you may be on a customer's premises. If so, try to have a look at the meeting room beforehand so that you can get the feel of it and, for example, establish where the power sockets are if you plan to use projection equipment.

At many functions, hospitable hosts will invite you to join them for a drink, possibly in a VIP area populated with people wearing so many symbols of office that you will think you are on a chain gang. Just remember the point in the chapter on nerves: be cautious in taking alcohol because, apart from the effect on your voice, it may also make you look florid and flushed. And put out cigarettes or cigars before you speak — you will look discourteously over-casual if you don't and, anyway, as the anti-smoking lobby becomes all-conquering, you may even find people walking out as you speak. If you are in a small group making a presentation to key customers and you light up without asking if they mind then you deserve to lose the sale.

If you get an opportunity, it may be worth cleaning your teeth and having a quick wash to freshen up before you speak. Talking of teeth, I suppose a really caring speaker would get bad ones fixed because they will be on display quite a lot; try out new false teeth before a speaking engagement and if they make you squeak or stumble over 's's' then go back to the dentist. Admittedly, you may feel this is all a bit over the top because public speaking isn't *that* important. Perhaps you are right — certainly, I don't think you should bother having a nose job.

If there is a break in the proceedings before you speak, it may be worth grabbing a breath of fresh air; as a further diversion I suppose you could take bets with yourself on how many times you will go to the lavatory — console yourself with the thought that even walking there and back may enliven you.

As it gets near to your time to speak, empty your pockets of bulky items because your clothes will look smarter. Check that your hair is tidy and ensure that all the right buttons and zips are fastened.

You should by this stage have a clear idea of the mood of the audience. This may depend on how well previous speakers have fared — if someone has made the audience sleepy or angry, your task may be more challenging. If they are very angry you may have to make a conscious effort to shift their minds by saying something like 'Yes, there's got to be a lot more debate about that, but I now want to talk about our export problems because unless we solve those...etc.

The mood at a dinner may depend on how freely the wine has flowed — too much and an audience may become 'brittle' and even mildly hostile, as it will if faced with an endless list of speakers (why will some organizers persist in this daft practice?). An audience can definitely 'go off' after an hour or two although, curiously, people sometimes get a second wind and switch on again — I once rose at 23.57 as the penultimate speaker at a marathon dinner and Les Dawson, who followed me at 'midnight plus two', went down a bomb. Anyway, irrespective of the time, if people are clearly out of control and throwing bread rolls, you will be wise to cut any whimsical references from your speech. If things are running very late, you may even have to be prepared to perform major surgery on what you planned to say.

Whatever the occasion, the obvious moral is to keep the audience in mind at all times. With experience you will 'feel' the atmosphere in a room and this will guide you as to whether, for example, to fillet out long, complicated anecdotes; you should certainly do so if things seem at all dead.

I know you will be fairly engrossed in your own build-up, but you still need to pay attention to what previous speakers say because you may want to rebut them or delete something from your own address to avoid duplication. If a previous speaker is an enormous success, well, you've done all you can so try not to be thrown off stride. Incidentally, listen for what is *not* said, too, and if no one else thanks the chef then maybe you should do so; you may score points as a considerate person.

Organizers can suffer from nerves too and this may sometimes make them over-anxious to get on with the speeches. Fine, *provided* any music has positively stopped (don't rely on a waiter saying 'We'll switch the tape off as soon as you start') and provided waitresses are not still moving about serving coffee or collecting cups. Suggest a little delay if this is happening or, better still, say 'When does the head waiter think his staff will be finished?'

The last stage in your countdown is slightly more

subjective, and it is to get yourself in the right mood. If, for instance, you know in your heart that you are a bit of a miserable 'so-and-so', well try to cheer up just this once. If you've had a rough time at the office or you are depressed because you didn't win the Reader's Digest prize draw, that's just too bad. Your audience simply won't want to know, so forget your problems for a moment, consciously change up a gear and *concentrate*. If you don't pay attention to what you are saying, your audience certainly won't.

CHECKLIST 10

☐ Are you properly dressed?

☐ Don't forget your notes.

☐ Allow ample time to reach the venue.

☐ Clear any open issues when you arrive, e.g. is it 'council' or 'committee'. Double check people's names.

☐ Stand where you will be speaking; check the public address system, podium, etc.

☐ Will the media be present?

☐ Plant a few questions.

☐ Find out who will be introducing you and what they plan to say.

☐ Establish what else will be happening — raffles and so on.

☐ Guard against too much hospitality.

☐ Before speaking, perhaps go outside for a breath of fresh air, even clean your teeth to freshen yourself up.

☐ Clearing your pockets of bulky items may make you look smarter.

☐ Try to assess your audience as a function progresses; note how other speakers are being received.

- ☐ Fine tune your words as your moment looms. Cut if the meeting is over-running or becoming unruly.

- ☐ Be sure any music has stopped and staff have stopped serving before you stand up.

- ☐ Get yourself in the right mood, think of your audience and *concentrate*.

11
BEING HEARD

One of the most important things to check at a venue is the public address system. For small face-to-face meetings you will be able to speak unaided, but for larger groups *you should use a microphone if you have any doubts about being heard.* Standing in an empty room beforehand, it may appear that you will be heard clearly. However, when you get to your feet, there may be movement and murmurs among your audience, clatter from a kitchen or a hum of sound from an adjacent room; any of these things may prevent your message getting across clearly. In addition, if you have to struggle to make yourself heard you will find it difficult to 'control' the audience and you may lose confidence and become more tense and hence less effective as a result. So, to repeat: if in any doubt, use a microphone.

Once you become used to them, neck or clip mikes are perhaps the best. You can hang them round your neck on a cord, or clip them to your lapel and then move around while speaking without your voice fading (because the microphone moves with you); but make sure you don't get tangled in the flex. At more elaborate conferences, instead of having a long flex, you may be wired up to a radio version with a transmission pack strapped in an intimate place.

Floor-standing microphones always make me feel as if I'm performing in cabaret, although they can be fine if stood alongside a lectern; microphones on table stands are perhaps better for after-dinner speakers. If you are speaking at a dinner in a room where a conference has been held you may be asked to speak from a lectern — possibly on a stage — which has been left *in situ*, or you may occasionally find yourself speaking from in front of the band. Neither is as ideal for an after-dinner speech as speaking from your dinner seat with a microphone on a table stand — but don't be too put off. If you've got something interesting to say you can speak from almost anywhere provided you can be seen. It helps to get an audience conditioned to where you are speaking from if the person introducing you speaks from there too, and this will probably make microphone arrangements easier, anyway. Wherever you are speaking from, try to avoid a long pause after you have been introduced while microphones are manhandled around.

Organizers should (but don't always) arrange to seat after-dinner speakers in a logical order so that a microphone can be passed along smoothly, and they should probably set the sound tone at the treble end for speakers. For business occasions, if you are not using a clip-on unit it may help to have microphones at both sides of a lectern so that your words will not be lost if you move your head to make eye contact with different sections of the audience. Avoid hand-held microphones if possible because you can get in a terrible tangle if you try to hold one and turn over notes at the same time.

If several speakers are to appear on a panel to answer questions, they *must* have a microphone each if the occasion is to flow smoothly. On no account be tempted to make do with one unit between two or three speakers because the pauses while people pass microphones backwards and forwards will kill any flow or cut-and-thrust. I have even seen panellists sitting comfortably on a sofa, then rising in turn to walk to a central microphone to answer 'spontaneous' questions — it was very obviously rehearsed and there was no sense of rapport. Incidentally, keep in mind that if you are answering questions the audience *must* be able to hear them. A central microphone positioned for questioners to use slows things down unless they queue at it, while passing microphones along rows of seats is not ideal; I must confess I have never seen the perfect solution. I've even seen sophisticated directional mikes that are pointed at questioners give trouble. It may on occasions not be a bad idea simply to ask questioners to speak up or even shout — this may even help inhibit critical members of an audience on robust occasions. Whatever system is in use, let me repeat: people must know what the question is if they are to understand your answer fully so, if all fails, repeat the question before answering it.

Ideally, you should try a microphone before using it and if you get the dreaded feedback then persist with any technicians until it is cured. Don't rely on a confident assurance that 'it will be OK'.

If you have no opportunity to try the public address system before using it, at least note how earlier speakers get on with the equipment.

If there is general chatter in a room before you start, do not blow into the microphone and say 'testing, testing', although there is no harm in a gentle tap on the microphone: you will be able to tell from the sound if it is live, while the audience may take the slight sound as a gentle indication that things are about to start. On other occasions turning down any background music, as well as lowering the lights, will send a similar signal to the audience.

Once you are in full flow, try not to knock the microphone. If one gives trouble (most likely with 'howl' due to poor positioning of microphones and speakers) or stops working altogether, your response will be governed by the size of the audience and the formality of the occasion. If it's a large gathering with a vital message to be put across, then you may have to say (loudly) that you will pause until the problem is solved. For smaller groups it may suffice to pitch your voice up and/or move from, say, a lectern on stage down among your audience so that they can hear you better. If it's an in-house function you could add some light-hearted comment about 'that's the last time we get (name of key rival) to run the technical side'. It's not easy but try not to be thrown by faulty equipment — a disruption which is handled well can actually add to an occasion. Once you resume your pitch you should try to give the audience time to settle down (as at the start of your speech) before hitting them with key points.

Check if someone is around who understands the equipment: there always should be for important functions (don't rely on the junior hall porter). Do beware of unguarded words in front of a live microphone; a mutter to the chairperson that 'they were a dim lot', as you sit down, may curtail your applause if the words boom out over the public address.

Before you speak, ask if any noisy heating or airconditioning fans can be turned off if they are distracting. Obviously, the same goes for any background music, tannoys, or phones in the meeting room; even the hum of a fridge behind a bar can be a distraction. Make a nuisance of yourself in stressing that this must be done because staff shifts change and it may get forgotten. I can't stress the point about the control of noise too strongly — I've introduced a panel of speakers only to have a loud band strike up in an adjacent room as the first question was asked, and I've been speaking when a phone has rung just behind me and — it became rather surreal — a waiter picked it up, called for Mrs X...who then stood by me and carried on a conversation about the weekly shopping with a relative! Memories are made of this. Wise organizers will check that no fire drills are to take place during a meeting, while if the doors squeak they will get them oiled so that latecomers don't distract the audience; if doors bang as they swing to then someone must be stationed at them to prevent the sound.

Having stressed the need to stop noise, I should perhaps mention that at times silence can be almost as distracting and, if prolonged, embarrassing. This means, for example, that if several people are to speak at a function the handover from one to another should be smooth and without awkward pauses. There will be occasions — such as prize-givings — when it will help things along if 'wallpaper' music is played to fill the silences as people walk up to collect their rewards; if you are the one presenting the awards then check that someone is on the volume control to turn the music down, or off altogether, if it is necessary for you to speak at any point.

A lot of attention to detail? Perhaps — but it is attention which can make the difference between a poor or average performance and a truly outstanding one.

Checklist 11

- [ ] If in any doubt, *use a microphone.*

- [ ] Practise with the equipment.

- [ ] Two microphones are desirable on a lectern if you are to move your head around.

- [ ] Check if someone is present who understands how the equipment works. There should be.

- [ ] Get extraneous noise (heating fans, etc.) stopped and check that any phones are disconnected before you speak.

- [ ] Don't knock a microphone when speaking.

- [ ] Have 'noise marshals' standing by to stop unexpected noise.

- [ ] Speakers on a panel should have a microphone each.

- [ ] An audience *must* be able to hear questions if answers are to mean anything.

- [ ] Remember that silence can be just as distracting as noise so, for instance, have background music playing if there is a long prize-giving.

12
STAND AND DELIVER

And, finally, it's cabaret time. You can't put it off any longer, you've done all the preparation you can, now it's time to deliver your speech or presentation. Let us start by repeating something from Chapter 10: consciously change up a gear and *concentrate*. If you are new to speaking you may find this difficult to believe, but it is actually possible to be in full cry yet find your mind wandering so that you almost become just another member of the audience. Obviously, this is a dangerous position to be in so put all your other problems to one side and concentrate on what you are saying.

Ideally, you should be standing to help command attention and I believe it is worth standing up if you are addressing more than just a small handful of people. Although you may be rigid with fear you should stand naturally, at least you should if your natural stance is fairly upright; if you slouch or hang your head (so that all people see is your bald patch) then you aren't really going to look as if you are enthralled about what you are saying. The manner in which you put your message across can make or mar it. Standing with your hands in your pockets may make you look so informal as to be uninterested in your topic, while you may be less convincing (or trusted) if you fail to make any eye contact with your audience.

Do try to move your eyes around the audience so that you involve all of them, rather than gaze the whole time at the rather attracive person in row three, but don't bob or weave about (unless of course they start throwing things); in other words, don't do anything that will distract an audience. And, as mentioned earlier in the book, don't attempt to use rehearsed gestures — they must be spontaneous. Wild arm movements may be riveting for a while but will become irritating if prolonged.

You won't go far wrong if you try to be as natural as possible. If, for instance, you are using notes or reading the whole thing, don't try to conceal the fact; after all, people are used to seeing presidents pull notes out of their pockets before talking when they step off a plane and royalty invariably read their speeches, so why not you?

TONE OF VOICE

By this stage it will be too late to do much about the content of your speech, but now is the time to be concerned about the *tone* in which you put it over. Use your normal voice (we hope this will not be too grating) because you will feel uneasy trying to change it, while if you try to talk 'posh' and aitches fall about all over the place your audience may be falling about too, with laughter. Don't worry about an accent unless you have a very pronounced one and are far from home, in which case you may need to slow down a shade so that people can understand you. Conversely, if you know that you usually speak rather slowly, you may need to speed up a little; people will hear faster than you speak and may guess the ends of your sentences before you get to them. This may tend to make them bored or impatient.

Don't try to speak at the same pace all the time

because you may sound monotonous if you do; you need highs and lows in a speech or presentation, the highs being the key points you wish to make, the lows being the linking sections in which you carry your audience from one high to the next. Even a judicious moment of passion or loss of temper over something will help keep people awake.

Obviously, the tone you use will depend on the occasion. You, and your audience, may be quite happy with a business presentation which is just read, but a warmer approach would be better for an after-dinner speech (with lectures and talks falling somewhere between the two). In general, your voice is likely to sound more natural if you either ad lib or speak from bullet points rather than read your words, because you will be more spontaneous. Whatever system you use, do steer clear of long sentences or you will run out of breath, and avoid sentences with the action verb right at the end or your audience may have difficulty following you.

Timing

Try not to babble away immediately you are introduced (nerves may make you tend to do this) but instead give people a moment to look at you before you start. Don't make the moment so long that it looks as if you have been struck dumb, otherwise the audience will get edgy. It seems to have become common for one presenter after another at a conference to start with 'Good morning (or afternoon), ladies and gentlemen'. This may sound courteous but it can sometimes introduce a mild jarring note because some of the audience may feel that they should respond, and in fact often do. But it rarely sounds enthusiastic or natural so I think you can safely skip the custom. What you should not do is say 'Good morning', get no response and then repeat more loudly 'I said good morning'. Not perhaps the best way to make friends if you hope to influence people.

Use pauses on occasions during your pitch, such as when you have fed them with statistics; if you are using visual aids you could look at a chart yourself with your audience and then, after a pause, say something like 'I've just realized that the figure there for your sales region is exactly ten times what it was five years ago'. Even though you may have planned such a comment in advance (though you should appear to ad lib rather than read it) it will add a spontaneity to your presentation that will help it along.

Use pauses too at other appropriate break points, for example: 'So, exciting results'...pause...'now let's turn to the new products we've got coming along'. Such pauses act rather like chapter headings in a book and give a moment for reflection (as does throwing in 'ladies and gentlemen' occasionally). That example also illustrates another thing you were advised to do in the chapter on preparing your words: build in signposts that tell your audience where you (and, you hope, they) are going. In saying 'now let's turn to...' you are clearly indicating that you are moving on to a new topic.

Don't hit your key message in your first few sentences but instead allow time for you and the audience to get used to each other. If, as sometimes happens, you have been given a hopelessly long-winded and effusive introduction, it may be worth ribbing yourself a shade before getting on to your message to show that you are not quite the pompous prat you were painted.

As you move to put across your main points, you must sound sincere — in fact, you must *be* sincere, as people may well sense if you are faking; you must make it clear that you believe in what you are saying, otherwise you won't convince an audience. However, avoid being so intense in your delivery that people consider you are either comic or demented; a reasoned approach is more likely to convince than a raving one. Incidentally, you may notice that advice in this book often falls into the 'on the one hand...on the other hand' category. This is because speaking and presenting is something of an art, not a science, and what may work for one speaker may not work for you. So, avoid the obvious pitfalls but try to be balanced and natural and use methods that appear to work for *you*.

After completing the main section of your speech, move on to your big finish: where appropriate, summarize or repeat your key points and, if you can think on your feet, re-emphasize anything based on the audience's reaction earlier — 'I know you're not convinced that we should have closed the Clacton depot but...'. If you are hoping that people will do something as a result of your address, make it clear exactly *what* you hope will happen, whether it's a 10 per cent increase in sales or a mass lobby of politicians or whatever. If action is needed, don't leave people in any doubt what that action is and what part they are expected to play. On other occasions you will not need to recap or call for action but simply, say, wish an association and its members well and then perhaps propose a toast.

AUDIENCE REACTION

So far, we have considered you and what you are saying and doing as the speaker. But there are more important people present: your audience. What are they doing? If you can hear the sound of marching feet then you can assume that you've lost them, while if you tell a joke and there is an embarrassed silence then you should avoid telling your other favourite. You will, with experience, be able to 'feel' how things are going. Even if you are just reading at a podium you should be able to judge from their posture and eye contact if people are following you; shuffling of feet and criss-crossing of legs should also be treated as alarm signals (the latter may, of course, be caused by physical rather than mental anguish if they have been sitting too long without a comfort break).

If people start talking while you are speaking then, while this is clearly ill-mannered, it is also an indication that you are boring them, perhaps through having spoken too long. It may be possible to pitch up your voice or a sympathetic toastmaster may step in and ask you to pause while he calls for 'the courtesy of silence for our guest' — if only one group is causing the noise then such an interjection will probably get applause from the rest as their way of indicating that they don't approve of the disruptive element. But... if noise does start up it means there is something wrong somewhere and the safest route is to cut things fairly short. If you lose an audience during an after-dinner speech then quickly sum up and shut up. Don't, whatever you do, try to 'fight' an after-dinner audience; if they want to be entertained and you want to educate them, you may be embarking on a lost cause. I've heard one speaker faced with background chatter stop and then say imperiously, 'I will continue when you are quiet'. Naturally, this simply increased the noise level so, idiotically, he said it again! And bear in mind that roof-raising applause at the words 'in conclusion' may be more ironic than anything else.

If you sense your audience is restless or bored while you are ploughing through a presentation where you are locked into lots of visuals, you may just have to slog on, although it may be worth trying an ad lib or two to liven the atmosphere. If an audience goes dead on you during a talk or lecture, consider shortening things and then invite questions (when the interest level may rise).

If you feel you will be too engrossed in what you are saying to be bothered about registering the vibes from an audience, then consider having someone at the back briefed to signal to you if you should shut up or if, say, a video is finally ready to be shown. You could even build in signals of your own so that when you use some particular phrase or sentence it means you are nearly through. If you signal to the audience by saying 'finally' or 'to sum up' then do keep your implied promise; don't grind on for another quarter of an hour. It is cruel to raise false hopes.

Ad libbing? I wouldn't do this deliberately until you have some confidence as a speaker, although there may be times when you simply have to ad lib, such as if you are speaking without notes and forget what you are planning to say next. If this happens, repeating what you've just said or saying 'let me sum up so far', and then doing so, will buy you time and, probably, remind you of what to say next.

You are unlikely to need to ad lib if you are speaking from bullet points or a full script, although if something significant happened earlier in the meeting you could look foolish if you don't mention it — if, for instance, you have a slide showing a product announcement date of 14 May and a previous speaker talked about 1 May, you may need to explain that one is the press release date, the other that of the sales launch. Occasionally, you may need to ad lib by summing up what you've said so far if a large number of latecomers arrive.

If a screen collapses or a pneumatic drill starts outside then you should make some reference (such as 'I think they're trying to train me as a police horse') but don't try to 'stage' such events, by asking a waitress, for example, to drop a plate at a particular point, because it is most unlikely that you will get the timing exactly right and things will appear false as a result.

On occasions you may need to ad lib because you are faced with a heckler or just a wag in the audience who passes an odd comment. I once saw a speaker stand up and start wringing his hands (remember the advice to guard against distracting mannerisms?) whereupon a wit asked 'Are you cold?' Happily this broke the ice, relaxed the speaker and actually improved the occasion. If you get a similar friendly interruption, you should smile to acknowledge it (you will appear churlish if you don't) but you don't have to respond and you should be cautious about turning the whole thing into a double act.

If interjections are more asinine or even hostile you should respond enough to show the audience that, like them, you know that you have a clown for company; your response need not be overly witty as almost anything will get applause from an audience wishing to show their disapproval of a heckler. Keep cool and try not to lose your temper with hecklers because audiences may swing behind them if you are too rude or overbearing. And avoid making martyrs out of hecklers — that might be their aim in attending in the first place.

Obviously, if the place is rioting before you are scheduled to speak then simply refuse to get up until the organizers have quietened things down (you may need to ignore this advice if it is your reputation as a person or as a speaker that has caused the problem).

To stop you worrying about hecklers, here are one or two more general things to keep in mind when you are on your feet:

- ☐ Even if you are reading everything else, don't read jokes because they need the 'lift' of spontaneity.
- ☐ Although women have countless advantages as speakers, some may have one disadvantage — a 'small' voice — and as a result they may need to speak more loudly than they normally would. In doing so they should guard against becoming strident.
- ☐ If you are talking about 'Point 1', 'Point 2' and so on, don't make the sections between the points too long or people will lose your thread. If one point has to be rather long then end it by saying 'so that's my first point, my second is...'.
- ☐ If lecturing, be sparing in using a pointer because doing so may mean you will keep turning away from your audience.
- ☐ Pause briefly if you are fortunate enough to get applause for a point you make, but don't make it obvious that you are expecting this at a specific point. If there is no response the sense of failure will be the same as if a joke falls flat.
- ☐ It is no bad thing to appear to be actually thinking about what you are going to say rather

than glibly trotting things out, provided your thought process isn't so long that people lose interest.
☐ Consider what you would do if your visual aid system collapsed. If the slide projector broke would you be able to get through your pitch by painting word pictures? Perhaps worth a moment's consideration.

TAKING QUESTIONS

Speakers are often expected to take questions at the end of a presentation so, if you plan to do so, mention this near the start or during your performance: 'I'll be happy to go into that aspect in more detail if you wish when I take questions later'.

Theoretically, questions should be put 'through the chair' if a chairperson is guiding the proceedings (and on these occasions, if questions are submitted in advance, they may be grouped together by the chairperson to avoid duplication) but this can slow things down so if in doubt handle questions direct. The most important but most neglected thing about questions is, as mentioned earlier, that *people must be able to hear them*. Obvious? Of course it is, yet so often speakers give erudite and charming answers that are meaningless because few have heard the question. This is partly because it is difficult to devise a public address system for questioners that doesn't slow things down as microphones are passed back and forth. Anyway, *repeat* any questions you are asked if there is any doubt about whether people have heard them, but *don't* change or shade their meaning. If someone asks 'Why did your company pollute the pond?' don't say 'The questioner has asked about water pollution' because he hasn't — he has asked about your particular shortcomings.

If you know that an awkward issue is certain to be raised, consider persuading a friendly soul to ask a question about it early in any questions session; it may be easier to handle than if it is raised in anger by someone later (although I'm not quite sure how you'd get out of your pond problem).

Don't lose your temper if asked difficult questions when you are making a pitch to potential customers. Anyone who buys something without asking searching questions may be a fool; a ruthless inquisition may be simply a search for knowledge as a prelude to buying. Anyway, if you can't handle questions you aren't properly briefed, are you? Handle questions convincingly and you will help your case.

On many occasions it is worth having a few questions planted in the audience to avoid an embarrassing hush when you call for questions, but your 'plants' should see if there are any spontaneous queries before jumping in, and they should not then laboriously read the questions you gave them. If you have an answer to a particular question that you know always goes down well, then have a signal to give to a friend to ask it so that you can end on a high note.

If genuine questioners raise irrelevant issues, don't rudely slap them down but offer to discuss their point later; for example, 'I know you're concerned about the problems you raise about your new car but, as people are here to discuss motor racing, I'm sure you won't mind if we leave your point until the interval when I'll discuss it with you and Mr Jones, the service manager'. That response successfully deflected a questioner who had attended a motorsport forum specifically to try to embarrass a dealer by raising the issue of his new car. Note that the response was perfectly friendly: a rather more curt 'that's got absolutely nothing to do with racing' would probably have inflamed the situation. As a further courtesy, jot down questioners' names — it will show how caring and aware you are if later you say 'as I mentioned earlier when replying to John Smith...'.

If you are answering questions as a member of a panel, don't whisper to your neighbour while others are responding to questions as this will appear discourteous; if you want to suggest to a fellow panellist that he or she could cover exports while you handle the domestic side, then a quick scribbled note passed along may be less distracting. Incidentally, you may need to be careful about leaving such notes lying around afterwards if they say things like 'tell that jackass that sales have doubled' or whatever. Do remember that bland agreement by panel members will become soporific — taking a different tack to the rest may liven things up.

Answering questions, either solo or as a member of a panel, is much easier than making a speech, but one word of caution: don't allow yourself to become indiscreet or your remarks may be slanderous. In fact, you need to keep legal affairs in mind whenever you are speaking. If you mildly rib someone, such as a colleague, while the butt of your humour is present, he or she might punch you but is unlikely to take you to court. However, if a cruel comment of yours is passed on secondhand the next day, then things could become more fraught. So take a little care.

You may have little to fear from having a lighthearted go at a well-known public figure (although some of them have started to bite the hands that have fed them the publicity they once craved) but, if you make a more vicious attack, you may not only end up in court but also find your audience swinging against you. You may discover the same thing happening (deservedly) if you use a lot of four-letter words; no legal action is likely to be taken against you for doing so, but if you rile or offend your audience you will have done enough damage already.

This is rather a long chapter, I know, but your actual delivery is the most important part of any speech or presentation. And, by the way, do know when to *stop* talking. You should have established in advance exactly what happens when you do stop, whether you hand back to the chairperson, introduce the next speaker, propose a toast or present a prize...whatever it is, just be sure you know.

Perhaps I should end the chapter by alerting readers to the fact that, with the increase in team-building meetings, 'games' may be played to get people together, or people sing on stage to backing tracks to break the ice. I pass on without comment an observation that the chief executives of the most successful companies seem to find pressing engagements before such musical frolics start.

CHECKLIST 12

- ☐ Concentrate.
- ☐ Stand up.
- ☐ Maintain eye contact with your audience.
- ☐ Take care with excessive arm movements.
- ☐ Be natural; be sincere.
- ☐ Use your normal voice. Women may have to speak up if they have a 'small' voice.
- ☐ Add light and shade to avoid sounding monotonous.
- ☐ Use pauses.
- ☐ Use 'signposts' to carry your audience along.
- ☐ If you have to shorten things, remember to get your key points over.
- ☐ Be specific if you call for action.
- ☐ Try to 'feel' how the audience is reacting.
- ☐ Handle questions direct rather than through the chair if it is a relaxed occasion.
- ☐ Don't lose your temper with difficult questioners.
- ☐ Know when to *stop* talking.

13
TAKING THE CHAIR

Those awful words 'chairperson' and 'chair' have been forced into use in this chapter because I haven't come across suitable alternatives. Women are just as effective in the chair as men, but our nomenclature hasn't yet caught up with current ideas on linguistic equality.

Those who take the chair and run a meeting, irrespective of its size, play a vital role because they can add an extra sparkle if they are good, and seriously damage a function if they are negligent in their approach.

If you speak regularly you could well find yourself 'in the chair', and it may be useful to consider the qualities needed to do this job. They are:

Reliability because the chair at least must turn up to the meetings.

Punctuality because the chair should start meetings on time.

Organizing ability because, even if someone else is doing the donkey work, a good chairperson will still double check that handout material is available, that the catering is functioning efficiently and so on.

Fairness because people will not be happy if they leave a meeting feeling they were denied a chance to have their say.

Tact because the lobbying before a committee meeting can be as important as what is said during the session, while the chair may sometimes have to referee between verbal sparring partners and may need to be diplomatic when doing so.

Firmness because meetings won't be effective if participants get out of control and sooner or later (preferably sooner) the chair may have to make it clear who is in charge in order to keep things on track.

If the above has scared you since you only borrowed the book because you've got to chair a small committee and you don't feel that you have all those listed qualities, then relax — neither do 90 per cent of chairpeople so there is no reason to feel you will be unable to cope. But an awareness and understanding of the job will help to make you that bit more effective when in the chair.

Obviously, the degree of application needed on the part of the chairperson will depend on the function. If you are chairing a *committee* then:

1 You should understand the written rules and regulations if it is a formal committee of, say, a trade association. Your right-hand man or woman — probably the association's secretary or legal adviser — should know them off by heart but you still need to know whether you as chair have a casting vote, how many people constitute a quorum and so on. Apart from anything else, if you have to keep referring to an official for rulings you will lose the respect of the committee members and as a result you will lose a little of the control you need over them.
2 You should understand the unwritten rules of a committee. Better to know in advance that a particular member of a trade association committee always responds in a certain way to a specific issue — such knowledge will help you to consider how to defuse, or deliberately use,

his or her predictable response. If you **are** chairing an inter-company function and it is known that any criticism of the delivery system induces apoplexy in the executive in charge of it, why not structure the agenda so that any such item comes when the rest of the meeting is out of the way? On a gentler note, if an elder statesman always likes to get in his little homily about the Home Guard, find a way of dissuading him from doing so *outside* not inside the meeting.

3 Start meetings on time and, if you do so with a gavel, bang it firmly and with confidence to stamp your mark on the session.

4 Keep control. If you let one person shoot off at a tangent you may lose the hearts and minds of the rest. Say at the start what is to happen at the meeting and then see that it does; it helps to have a timed agenda (for you, even if not for everyone) with an estimate of the amount of time each item will take. Sum up at intervals (rather like the 'signposts' it was suggested you put into a speech) to indicate where things are heading: 'So it's agreed we take a stand at the exhibition. Now under agenda item 3, let's consider organization'. That example illustrates another duty of the chair: to see that things are discussed in the right order. Don't let a committee discuss who is going to organize an exhibition until it has been agreed that there should actually *be* one. Needless to say, the construction of an agenda needs care. If you put a controversial item first there may not be time to discuss anything else although the subject will at least get a thorough airing; if you put it last, an approaching lunch break may encourage more dynamic decision making. Once again: your choice.

The same approach may be needed if you are chairing a *conference*. If it is a major affair there will obviously be people making it all happen but you still need to be 'aware' — aware, for instance, that the projectionist's glazed look means that he isn't really sure that the slides are in the right order and would like another five minutes to check. And aware enough too to ensure that the catering staff are alerted if things are running late and coffee will have to be delayed if it is not to be cold.

If, as the chairperson, you have to introduce several conference speakers then say enough about each one to establish their credentials (unnecessary, of course, if they are all well-known to everyone) and 'bridge' their presentations to carry the audience along: 'So Penelope's told us about distribution, now Bill's going to talk about after-sales service...'. If material is to be handed out after a meeting then say so at the start so that people don't waste time making notes.

If you are chairing a less elaborate function at which someone is to give a *talk* or *lecture*, then you may need to take a more relaxed approach to timing, if, for instance, people are straggling in, and you will obviously not need to be so overtly 'in control' as at a committee meeting or a major conference. Your role will be more that of host and as such you should make people welcome and then move on to introduce the speaker. It seems elementary courtesy to me for a chairperson to *ask* people how they want to be introduced, but not all do. If you don't check, there is a reasonable chance that you may be working from an out-of-date biography; if you announce that a speaker is a banker and he starts by saying that he has had a change of heart and become a baker you, as the chair, will be the one with yeast on your face. So check. Having done so, and also found out what someone is going to talk about, *don't* then give the talk for him. And don't grind your particular axes on a subject when introducing a speaker, although by all means highlight why the talk is relevant: 'At the moment, only a few of us face this problem, but in five years it will affect all of us, which is why we're so lucky to have Trevor here to talk about it today'.

If questions are to be taken after a talk then theoretically they should be put through you, as the chair, but if a speaker has gone down well and clearly knows what he is about, just thank him for his splendid talk and say 'I'm sure Trevor will now be happy to take your questions'. Of course, if you say that and no one asks anything, it will all fall a shade flat so *always* prime one or two people beforehand to ask something — this is much better than a long pause while you wrack your brains for a question. Questions are better coming from the floor anyway because if the chairperson asks one it tends to highlight the fact that the meeting is being padded out.

If a speaker is likely to have a rough ride from the audience then, *mon brave*, I'm afraid you as chairperson will have to share the firing line and ask for questions to be addressed to you; if so, don't attempt to soften or shade them. As mentioned earlier in the book, if people haven't heard the question then you or the guest speaker *must* repeat them. Too often a chairperson and a speaker get involved in a fascinating exchange with someone on the front row — fascinating, that is, to those around them but meaningless (and rude) to the rest. Never let one person hog all the questioning, by the way.

Wise chairpeople will have secret signals to indicate to helpers that things are about to end (so that they can get the hot pies ready) or, more urgently, that a question on a 'safer' topic is needed to calm the proceedings. Of course, I am not suggesting that you should totally manipulate things with planted questions and secret signals. Oh, I don't know though.

If things get really out of hand with an unruly audience, it is your job as chair to protect any speakers (metaphorically rather than physically, I hope) by banging your gavel, calling for order and, if necessary, suspending the meeting or ejecting trouble makers. Organizers of a function are, temporarily at least, 'the occupiers' of the premises where it is held and can therefore decide who may attend. Even if people turn up in response to advertisements and are therefore legally present, you can still ask them to leave if their behaviour justifies it. 'Threatening, abusive or insulting words' may amount to behaviour likely to cause a breach of the peace, which is an offence, as it is to create a disturbance to prevent the completion of business at a lawful public meeting. If people don't leave when asked they are trespassers and you are allowed to use 'reasonable force' to eject them. But try a diplomatic approach first and stop worrying — it very, very rarely happens.

Incidentally, if you have to chair a *panel* featuring several people who have previously made individual presentations to the group, it may be worth briefly (and fairly) summarizing what they said before inviting questions: 'Well, ladies and gentlemen, John has told us about the challenges the new legislation will pose and what we can do about them, Jane has taken us through the insurance issue and suggested a solution, and Ron has explained the tax side and given us three ways of avoiding paying. I'm sure you've got plenty of questions for them. Would somebody like to start?' Note the use of first names here — I think this makes things friendlier although it could be inappropriate on formal occasions. Up to the chairperson's judgement — see why they need to be 'aware'? Just as they do over dress — if you are chairing a meeting in a very hot room then people may look to you to suggest they may like to remove their jackets.

Incidentally, if you chair a panel you must be fair and give every member a chance to speak. Mind, don't forget that a bit of cut-and-thrust will be more entertaining than bland agreement; you may even provoke disagreement to liven things up a little. If panellists have appeared together before they may well have 'set pieces' that they will launch into if fed the right question or cue. If things are slow-moving the chair should push the debate along when moving from one panellist to another: 'Claire has answered the legal side but, John, have you any views on the moral issue?' The chair may need to remind panellists what the actual question was, so it is a wise move to jot each one down.

If you are chairperson at a *dinner*, *dinner-dance*, *banquet*, or *ball* (the last two are really the same as the first two, but using the best china) you are more than ever the host, and you should be a convivial one. But don't let the conviviality lead you to neglect your duties. You should still be alert for disasters with the catering and you should be watching for the arrival of any after-dinner speakers; you should then make them welcome and try to put them at ease (they are likely to be more nervous than people scheduled to make straightforward business presentations). Liaise with the caterers and toast-master or master of ceremonies over timing: 7.30 for 8.00 usually means starting at 8.15. It may be tempting to let a pre-dinner drinks session run on if it is obviously going well, but resist this temptation if doing so will mean a carefully planned timetable being thrown out of kilter and speakers being introduced so late that people would prefer to dance or go home.

It should be up to the chair to decide whether to have a break before speeches at the end of a meal; the decision will probably be influenced by the average age of the audience, but it should be noted that it is better to say 'There will be a short break and the speeches will start promptly at 9.30' than 'There will now be a 10-minute break' because they may be straggling in for ages with the less precise approach. However well disciplined an audience, if you have a break you will invariably have to plead for people to take their seats — one or two people always seem to stand chattering when everyone else is waiting for the speeches.

At the end of a meal, ensure that serving staff have finished before you start the speeches. Unless things have been carefully worked out in advance with the caterers, you run the risk of staff serving liqueurs while people are speaking; even if the staff are quiet, their moving around the room and their murmured 'Was yours the port?' will distract an audience. Even worse, it's been known for cash to be collected during speeches with altercations breaking out.

When speakers finish, lead the applause — this is sometimes slow to start if people have risen to drink a toast; if, of course, you think a speaker deserves a standing ovation then stay on your feet to encourage others to follow suit. On a less happy note, I'll have to leave it to you to decide what to do about a speaker who drones on, and on, and on. Perhaps push a note under his nose?

I hope it is unlikely that you will need to eject unruly folk from functions but don't forget that drink may make people 'tired and emotional'; if you know that someone in a group gets a bit wild after a glass or two, consider nominating a 'minder' to keep a watchful eye on him. Don't drink too much yourself, of course, because you need to keep your wits about you right to the end of the evening, as you do in fact to the end of any function you chair — you should be the one to see that a civic dignatory or other VIP, such as a visiting national president, is properly thanked and escorted from the premises.

And I'm sorry, but your duties as a chairperson don't end when the function does. Don't forget to write to thank people. Consider what follow-up action is needed; for instance, are minutes to be sent out? How can the event be improved next time? Is it time to resign?

Decisions, decisions.

CHECKLIST 13

- [ ] Be realistic as a chairperson.
- [ ] Be punctual. Start meetings on time.
- [ ] Be organized.
- [ ] Be fair and tactful.
- [ ] Be firm. Keep control of the occasion.
- [ ] Don't worry if you are not all of the above — few chairpeople are.
- [ ] Know the formal rules for your organization.
- [ ] Know the unwritten rules too.
- [ ] Give a meeting a sense of priority, e.g. decide *whether* to hold a function before discussing *when*.
- [ ] Check your facts before introducing speakers; don't give their presentation for them when doing so.
- [ ] Ensure people are ready to listen before introducing speakers.
- [ ] 'Protect' speakers if a meeting gets out of hand.
- [ ] Ensure the audience hears any questions being answered; if in doubt: repeat them.
- [ ] Develop a system of signals to your support staff.

- ☐ Watch the timetable, Don't prolong the drinks session for a dinner if it throws the timing and the catering out.

- ☐ Before relaxing after a function, consider how it can be improved next time.

14
INTERVIEW TECHNIQUES

In an earlier chapter you were cautioned against becoming over-relaxed, and hence indiscreet, when answering questions after a speech or presentation. The caution applies even more when being questioned by someone from the media; while at the time you may only be 'speaking in public' to one person, namely the interviewer, you will be reaching many more people when the interview is published or broadcast. However, don't get over-anxious because most interviewers are simply seeking information and will be perfectly polite; you just need to be alert because abrasive interviewing techniques seen on TV, and the intense competition between media outlets, may occasionally encourage a more searching approach. This may come as a shock to you particularly if, as the boss, you are usually surrounded by sycophants and lead a slightly sheltered life. The situation isn't helped by the fact that business people are not necessarily liked or trusted and there may even be mild hostility, especially towards what is seen as 'big business'. Just accept it all as an introduction to the real world and try not to lose your temper, because the result, while riveting viewing or listening, may not help your cause or company.

Anyway, with the recognition that you will probably be interviewed at some stage in your business career, let us start with a few general points, applicable whether the approach is from the press, radio or TV. And the first point is that no law *compels* you to agree to an interview and there may be times when it would be foolish or risky to do so — such as if you are within 24 hours of completing the final details of a delicate factory closure. But, and it is a fairly hefty 'but', such news tends to escape and your refusal to speak may be seen as confirmation of people's worst fears. What does 'no comment' usually convey to you? That's right, that the speaker has something to hide. Nevertheless, there may be times when it is better to have an announcer say 'We asked ABC Company to send a spokesman but they declined' than to turn up and get a thorough mauling. Occasionally, it may be possible to have one specific area put 'out of bounds' before agreeing to be interviewed but you need to be very sure of the journalist when negotiating this. Of course, if a crisis hits your company which directly affects the public — if you operate a fleet of ships and one sinks, for instance — then you simply won't get away without being interviewed, and nor should you want or expect to do so. At such times you will wish that you had done what any sensible company does, namely 'crisis planning', in which you consider 'worst case' scenarios; such planning may lead you to the conclusion that you, as the boss, haven't necessarily got the best TV manner and that someone else in the company should be the spokesperson. Whoever is chosen to be the spokesperson in the event of an emergency should rehearse by being fed with every awkward question his or her colleagues can think of.

A crisis may also make you wish that you had done another thing sensible companies do: built good links with the media, with someone in the company clearly in charge of public relations. You aren't too bothered about public relations in your company? How quaint; I hope you can still get supplies of quills for your clerks' pens. At a time when politicians conduct almost their whole lives with the media in mind, and when many industries are under scrutiny from conservationists, environmentalists and many other 'ists', it is foolish not to take public relations seriously. If you do then you should have far fewer fears about being interviewed.

As with public speaking, the key to a successful interview is to know your subject and to *think*: if you are relocating your factory, for example, realize that good news for Town A (to which you are moving) may be bad news, and mean job losses, for your present Town B. These are the times when the public relations officer needs to be carefully coordinating who says what and when, ideally with a 'Q & A' supplied to all concerned, listing anticipated media questions and suggested answers so that everyone in the company sings the same song. Such song sheets should not be left around for the media to find, otherwise you may alert them to things they wouldn't otherwise have thought of. Clearly, you should not commit *anything* to paper that you would be unhappy to see appear in a newspaper or courtroom later.

Whatever the interview, unless it is for a trade journal, remember that you will probably be reaching a general audience so avoid 'business-speak' and any industry jargon that will be incomprehensible. Above all, remember that your *manner* will be as important as your message. This is obvious on radio and TV where your tone of voice conditions what impression people have of you, but if you adopt an overbearing approach with the press, well...you can't expect them to strive to be too sympathetic towards your case in their reports, can you?

PRESS

If you are to be interviewed by a journalist from a newspaper or magazine, it is sensible to brief yourself about the publication. Is it trade or consumer oriented? What is the circulation? How important is it? (This may sometimes be in inverse proportion to its circulation if it is, say, a key trade journal.) Do you advertise in it? Know this last information *not*, please not, so that you can ask or hint for favourable treatment because you are an advertiser, but simply so that you don't appear ignorant of your company's advertising policies if the subject crops up.

Incidentally, if one or two publications are absolutely key to your company, try not to give the others the impression that you regard them as second-rate makeweights; if one of them turns hostile it could make life difficult for you, so why take the risk? Politeness isn't expensive.

Don't neglect free newspapers and magazines but do remember that many magazines may have longish lead times if you are hoping for an interview to appear around the time of the launch of a new product. And with any publication be cautious in trying to go 'off the record'. If the news is hot enough the request may be ignored, while you will destroy your credibility with your regular press contacts if you try going off the record too often (as you will if you abuse press embargoes). Be equally cautious in trying to embargo news too, that is, asking or expecting the media to hold a story until a specific date. Journalists in many countries already virtually disregard embargoes and few of them will cooperate with you anywhere if you abuse such requests.

Your search for accuracy in what is written about you and your company will be helped if you have accurate press releases available together with relevant photographs; if any of the latter are of you then they should be fairly recent — don't try to camouflage your real age.

RADIO AND TV

Your presentation needs to be even more thorough if you are interviewed for radio or TV because, if you flounder, your inadequacies may be cruelly exposed. If you are interviewed during or immediately after you have called a press conference, it will be obvious why you have been approached, but if you are invited to a studio to take part in a programme then conduct a little research. Consider whether you have been invited because they genuinely want to hear your views or because you are being set up as the 'fall-guy' to face a host of hostile environmentalists, customers or whatever — the knowledge that you are being set up need not stop you appearing, but it should prevent you being too casual in your approach. Studying a previous edition of a programme may give you a guide to its flavour and whether the approach is likely to be gentle or tough; finding out who else will be appearing with you should also provide a clue. Establish too if it will be a live or recorded programme; there may be advantages in the former because you run no risks from misguided editing or the humiliation of finding that your erudite responses have been cut to a 15-second clip.

Whatever the programme, do arrive in plenty of

time because you may not perform well if you are still panting after rushing from the car park. Use the time before the programme *not* to accept any alcohol offered but to get names right; if the interviewer is called Tom, make a mental or written note of it then you won't keep calling him Tim. But don't be the one to start using first names when an interview starts; if you say 'Well now, Tom' and he replies 'Yes, Mr Brown', his use of 'Mr' will sound a mild snub even if not actually intended as such.

Cancel bells, buzzers or bleepers on any hi-tech equipment you carry around to show the world what an important fellow you are and then, when you move into the interview arena, expect to be given a question or two so that the sound man can check the level of your voice. At first you may find it mildly embarrassing to list what you had for breakfast, or whatever else you are asked, but respond properly to help the sound people because it is in your interest that your voice comes across well. And just as suggested for delivering a speech, use your normal voice, don't try to change it or pose.

As well as being asked a trivial question to check sound levels, you may also be given an outline of the questions you may be asked; leading figures who need to be coaxed onto some programmes are able to lay down precise ground rules and vet all the questions in advance. But let us assume that you are not yet in that exalted category so if the interviewer says 'I'll just outline why you're here and then ask you how big the new factory is and what you'll be building there', don't relax and think how easy it is all going to be because, as you preen when answering what you think is the final question, dear old Tom may then throw you by asking 'So you're going to be importing even more components from

Korea, which will mean job losses here'. Possible collapse of stout party (you) unless you are on your toes. So stay alert.

If you know there may be an awkward question around it may be wiser to pre-empt it by getting the bad news out of the way when referring to the good: 'Of course this means we'll be importing more components from Korea, but we're working with our local suppliers to increase *their* production too and, for us, the net effect will be an increase in jobs'. If, as is likely, the interviewer isn't following your replies too closely and then later asks the awkward question, you can then reply, 'Well, as I mentioned a few moments ago....etc'.

If a programme is being recorded you may be loved if you answer in 'sound bites', that is short self-contained summaries that can be used on their own. You can do this by building the question into your reply; if asked 'How many jobs will the new factory mean?', don't say 'Twenty-seven' but 'The new factory will mean twenty-seven new jobs'.

Remember you are there for your information or views, which means being a little more forthcoming than just saying 'yes' or 'no', which may make you sound curt. Try to come over as a pleasant person that people can trust. However, this doesn't mean you allow yourself to be browbeaten or railroaded — if the interviewer makes a glaring error about your affairs then correct it; if *you've* made an error, then admitting it may make you seem much more frank and honest. Remember that if you have given an answer and there is then a silence, you don't have to fill it, so don't. Leaving pauses is a well-known interviewing technique and the hope is that you, feeling uneasy at the silence, will fill it with an indiscretion. Obviously, if there is an area you are simply not prepared to discuss under any circumstances, then this must be agreed before you go on air. If you are likely to be interviewed regularly on delicate issues then study how politicians bob and weave and avoid actually answering questions, all the while giving the impression they are desperately honest and earnest.

Don't bang on anything while on radio or TV (the thumping may spoil the programme) and don't 'bang on' either in trying to plug a product too much because, even if you get away with it, it is likely to irritate the audience and it won't help your chances of being asked back. Don't drone on too long or get sidetracked when answering a question. The advice is often given to 'get your point across at all costs'. Of course you should, but use a hefty dose of common sense in doing so; if you are being asked about major job losses, you will appear an uncaring idiot if you keep switching to discuss the fact that you have changed the logo on your label. Don't strive to be funny but do try to develop a sense of time — really experienced people wait until they know there are 30 seconds or so of an interview left before launching their key missile, safe in the knowledge no one will be given time to deflect it.

One last point affecting both radio and TV: if you become a well-known figure — such as an industry leader — turn down invitations to appear on panel programmes covering worldly issues if you know in your heart that doing so will expose your ignorance of matters other than purely business ones. A few business reputations have been damaged through people not following this advice.

Radio

All the above applies to both radio and TV. Don't neglect the former because there may be countless opportunities to project yourself and your company on local radio; you could even practise on hospital radio although this is perhaps a shade unfair on the serious cases.

Two other points on radio:

☐ If you are scheduled to appear on a phone-in programme then alert colleagues or friends to stand by ready to call, either to avoid embarrassment for you if there are no genuine questions, or to ring in with an easy one if you are having a rough time from other questioners. If you then recognize the caller don't make this obvious or your subterfuge will be exposed.
☐ Your clothing won't be seen so it doesn't really matter what you wear, although it is perhaps sensible not to have anything tight around your throat, such as a collar or the hands of a distraught public relations colleague.

TV

Clothing will be much more critical if you are appearing on TV because how you dress will condition what sort of person viewers perceive you to be. If you sport pince-nez and a silver-topped cane, or wear suede shoes and a revolving yellow bow tie, then you are 'saying' something about yourself to viewers (only good breeding prevents me saying what it is). Just give some thought to dress: if you appear on a panel and are the only one dressed formally, with everyone else in casual clothes, then you have already positioned yourself as 'the business person'. I am not suggesting that this is wrong; clearly, it would be absurd for the elderly chairman of a major company to appear uneasily on screen in a jokey tee shirt. I am just recommending that you should at least think about what to wear so that you don't look out of place.

Don't smoke on TV and don't bob about so that you distract viewers. Look at the interviewer rather than the camera; on no account try to do both otherwise you will appear shifty. Above all, keep in mind with TV, more than with any other medium, that the impression you give may be as important as any message; viewers may not (in fact probably won't) remember the latter but they will remember whether you seemed like a person they could trust.

To help you to project yourself properly, you may consider going on a training course. Many are available and, if nothing else, they will get you accustomed to seeing yourself on screen and give you experience in handling awkward interviews. Worthwhile for those expecting high visibility on TV but for lesser mortals an in-house programme, much the same as suggested earlier for speech making, should suffice. To add a little spice, ask a friendly local radio or TV man (and every company should have one) to come in and grill people. Caution: remember the advice for press conferences and don't let such grilling sessions lead you to assume that all interviewers will be hostile; if you get so fired up that you bite the interviewer's head off in answering the first question, you will not come over as the caring and compassionate person we all know you really are. Recording any radio or TV programmes you appear on, and then studying them at leisure, could help you to improve your techniques.

With practise and experience, who knows, you could become an adept and frequent interviewee. If so, it is worth mentioning that there can be mild problems if just one person in a company has a high visibility and good media contacts — for the person concerned there may be jealousy from less visible colleages, while for the company, if the person leaves then the charisma and media contacts leave too. If you become the spokesperson of your company then be careful to clear with the appropriate authority just what you can say, stressing that too many 'no go' areas will make you appear shifty when interviewed. Sadly, too many executives fail to understand public relations and expect every word in an interview to be accurate and favourable. If you are in the firing line you need to make it clear to collegues that no one should demand or expect 100 per cent success rate. Overall impressions are what the public take away. It isn't easy handling interviews on a sensitive issue and no one should be crucified for the occasional mishap.

And if an interview goes hopelessly wrong? Well, what was the headline in your newspaper yesterday? What was the item immediately after the break in the evening television news? You probably can't remember because people forget fleeting news very quickly, so don't worry too much if you drop a mild clanger — the bell will not be tolling for the sinking of your career.

CHECKLIST 14

- [ ] No law forces you to be interviewed — but 'no comment' may be taken as a sign of guilt.

- [ ] Build good links with the media.

- [ ] Crisis plan — consider 'what if' scenarios.

- [ ] Prepare by having awkward questions thrown at you by colleagues.

- [ ] Consider why *you* are the one being interviewed. Are you being set up as the 'fall-guy'?

- [ ] Brief yourself about the newspaper or programme.

- [ ] Is the programme live or recorded?

- [ ] Don't try to embargo trivialities.

- [ ] Allow plenty of time to get to the interview.

- [ ] Avoid pre-interview drinks.

- [ ] Don't pose; don't patronize; don't lose your temper.

- [ ] Avoid 'business-speak'.

- [ ] If an interview is going well, beware of the last awkward question.

- [ ] You don't have to be the one to fill any silences in an interview that is becoming difficult.

- ☐ Speaking in 'sound bites' may help get your comments used on air.

- ☐ Don't try to hide mistakes or bad news — assume you'll be found out.

- ☐ Try to get your points across even if the interviewer gets sidetracked.

- ☐ If you are to appear on phone-in programmes alert colleagues to be ready to call if things are slow or the going gets rough.

- ☐ Your clothing and your manner are important on TV — how you are perceived may be as important as your words.

- ☐ Consider a training course — if nothing else, conduct an in-house one, perhaps using local journalists to help.

- ☐ If it all goes wrong remember: memories are short. Don't over-react.

15
BEHIND THE SCENES

If you make fairly frequent business presentations or after-dinner speeches, it is likely that you will eventually become embroiled in *organizing* such functions. Even if you don't, you will become a more 'aware' performer if you understand something of what goes on behind the scenes, so while by no means being exhaustive (or, I hope, exhausting) the next three chapters cover some of the essentials that go to make a successful function.

ORGANIZATION

Success obviously hinges on organization and the key is that one, and only one, person *must* be in overall charge; one person must be pulling all the threads together. The chosen organizer must have sufficient clout and support to make things happen within a company because the job calls for determined decision making, often at short notice. You are a one-person business? Congratulations — it's you, so find a quiet moment between filling in government forms to consider just what is involved. Larger organizations may have someone who specializes in arranging meetings, which means they build up a knowledge of venues, speakers and so on; more often — but less satisfactorily — things are handled on an *ad hoc* basis with each department looking after its own affairs.

Companies may consider using outside organizations to arrange important presentations. There are plenty of them about but in the main they are not very large so it is unfair to waste their time and money in pitching for your business unless you are serious about using them; don't just interview them in order to pinch their ideas. And don't be seduced by glamorous videos of major conferences they claim to have organized. Instead, think carefully about whether they seem the sort of people you will find it easy to work with — personal chemistry can make an important contribution to a successful event (and personality clashes can seriously damage one). Are there many staff involved or is it really just a one-person set-up? There may be no harm in the latter, but you should at least be aware of it. If your business makes a lot of presentations, there may be merit in commissioning one outside company to do all such work for, say, one or two years. You don't change advertising agents for every ad you run, so why change conference organizers? However, do keep a close watch on costs and don't allow the relationship to get so cosy that it becomes inefficient or stale; take care, for instance, if the company you commission in turn commissions other supporting companies (who in turn...) that not too many percentage pluses have been added to invoices before you pay them.

If you do decide to use an outside organization to arrange a function then establish clear lines of communication into your company as well as equally clear payment terms. And don't look for 'yes-men' because you are, or should be, paying them for their advice, so listen to it. Should several companies be involved in your meeting (covering such things as lights, catering and so on) then do make sure they are liaising properly; things will probably work best if one company is made responsible for the rest.

The back-up support needed for the organizer-in-chief will obviously depend on the size of the meeting; a typist may be needed to prepare name badges, someone to sign in guests, and so on; it should be established when commissioning outside companies which of such things they will handle.

Noise

Almost any size of meeting requires 'noise marshals', for example to stop kitchen staff from chattering in the next room while you are building up to your big finish. I was once attempting to give a fairly serious presentation in one section of a hotel room which had been divided up, when a band struck up next door; I began to despair when I saw my audience's feet tapping and gave up when two people started dancing. I am not sure you are going to believe this but, while finishing this book, I described the above incident to the chairman during a dinner at which I was due to speak. I idly raised the point simply because we were in a similar subdivided hotel room. We finished coffee, he introduced me, I stood up and (you've guessed it) just as I began, the music started, very loudly, next door. *So do have noise marshals.* (In this instance I was probably as much to blame as the outside company involved in the organization because I should have asked if anything was booked for the adjacent section.)

You may think I'm becoming boring about the noise issue but it really is the single most disruptive factor in meetings, so do pay attention to stopping any distracting sounds.

For presentations with more than a handful of people, you may need a master of ceremonies to make general announcements and marshal guests; choose someone with a strong voice and enough confidence to announce that the projector has broken and the coffee break is being brought forward without giving the impression that the function has collapsed. For more formal groups, a toastmaster will add a touch of class; if you use the same one every time he — or very rarely she — will get to know your company personnel and be more efficient as a result; your company speakers may be more confident too, knowing they are in familiar hands. Take care to spell out exactly what you want a toastmaster to do and, particularly important, *say*, because some of them are 'characters' (they would hardly be doing the job otherwise) and the sight of an audience may encourage them into thespian touches you could do without.

But back to the person in charge. The first thing you should do is draft an outline programme with rough timings and brief details of who will be covering which subjects if there are several speakers. When you have a programme that seems to work logistically, go back to your objectives to see if they will be met, and then — here we go again — think of your audience. Will the programme meet their expectations?

Don't be stuffy in your planning. If you've been running an annual function in a certain way for several years, that may be a good enough reason for a change. Is the company booming? If so, why not move to a more upmarket venue or spend an extra day on the meeting? However, do watch the 'escalation factor'; if you go to a three-star hotel one year and a four-star the next, guests may expect five-star treatment the year after. The same caution applies to visual effects and celebrities; if you lay on a lavish sound and light show with television stars for the facelift of a fridge, what icing can you put on your brand new model when you launch it next year?

If you hope to have information flowing two ways (and in these enlightened times you should), consider splitting up a presentation, say with service repair staff meeting in one room, sales personnel in another. Perhaps start with them all in one room for a general presentation before separating and then coming together again at the end for an uplifting address from the boss. The choice of venue will be critical in such cases and you must watch traffic flow along corridors; timing will be important too to avoid one group hanging around while another more long-winded session grinds to an end. A 'holding' area may be useful.

When you have settled your outline programme (incidentally, if necessary, get it cleared on high before going much further with the arrangements), consider an appropriate title for the presentation. 'Into the nineties' and 'Forward for success' are totally meaningless, though often encountered, and are at least better than just calling something 'a presentation'. But try to be more original.

THE PROGRAMME

Whether organizing the function yourself or using an outside team, *allow plenty of time*. Even then there will be last-minute panics. In fact, if you are not feverishly trying to change a slide with an hour to go, perhaps your subject matter has gone stale. However, do get the basic organization off the ground as soon as possible; if you don't, you may find for instance that the most suitable venue is already fully booked.

Keep the audience in mind and plan the timetable to suit them as much as yourself. I once spoke at a dinner where the chairman introduced 12 people on the top table with a detailed biography of us all — jobs, hobbies, the lot — and the audience simply didn't want to know. The chairman felt he was doing the right and polite thing, but in attempting to flatter 12 people he went on so long that he irritated 450 others and came very close to wrecking the function.

While considering timing, don't arrange a meeting during a peak selling period or call in the salesforce for a function if you've just set them tough targets. Don't arrange to call on a customer in the afternoon if you know he imbibes at lunch and becomes tired and emotional, and don't call breakfast meetings if people have long distances to travel.

And still on timing, don't make your schedule too tight. You need to strike a balance between hustling people around and being so relaxed that they feel you are wasting their time. Allow for bad weather and late arrivals in winter and for security checks and baggage delays if air travel is involved. The latter may also affect the metabolism of delegates, so give them time to adjust before hitting them with an important message.

The time of day will, or should, affect when you schedule key presentations. If you want to imply that the company is in deep trouble, don't do so immediately after a lunch where wine is served; the audience may just let your words wash over them.

When you have juggled with your draft timetable,

before putting it into effect bounce it off someone fairly typical of your proposed audience. At the very least, show it to a colleague or friend to get a fresh opinion.

Finally, before you set your programme in stone, have another think through it yourself. In particular, consider whether all the various strands mesh together. One area which needs careful planning is transport because the perils are obvious if there are delays or confusion. If you need to hire coaches to move delegates, then search for a reliable firm and check that drivers know exactly where they have to go (I've spent a wasted evening being driven around San Francisco because a badly briefed driver simply failed to find a venue). If you need more than one coach they should be clearly numbered, and guests should be reminded to note which coach they are on. They should also be told if it is safe to leave coats, briefcases, etc. on board during any stops. Try to arrange for staff with umbrellas to be on hand to escort people from coaches to venues if it is raining.

Once a programme is agreed, *write it down*, showing the time something happens, what happens and, above all, who is responsible for making it happen. Send copies of the timetable to all concerned, not forgetting the manager and head waiter at your venue. During the event itself ask someone to mark the actual times on a copy of the timetable so that you build up experience for the next function.

FINANCE

Meetings cost money, and a lot of it if you let creative people get out of control, so it is vital to budget as carefully as for any other aspect of business life. However, I would plead with financial men to recognize that flexibility may be needed 'on the day' when, for instance, cash may work wonders in solving problems in getting something done quickly. Accountants should not tie organizers down too tightly with their beloved systems and controls.

If you are calling on a client to make a presentation on a product, the cost of the trip will be part of your normal business expenses, but for more elaborate meetings the organizer should sit with the company's official keeper of the cash to draw up a budget; major conferences may require a separate cost centre. By the way, there is a coconut for any reader who can provide a *rational* reason why conference guests should have to queue at hotel checkouts to settle 'incidentals', like phone calls, separately and then, invariably, claim them back on their expenses. I refuse to believe there is a sensible reason but the situation invariably seems to occur.

Always consider your fixed costs first — hire of room and projector, fees for outside speakers, etc. Then itemize the variable costs — meals, drinks, presentation folders and so on. If your draft budget is frightening, you could consider scaling down the presentation or at least switching it to a smaller and cheaper venue, but remember there may be cancellation charges from the original place.

If you are involved in international events with several nationalities, your budget may need to allow for special signs as well as interpreters, who are not cheap. Try to find people who understand your trade jargon and remember that half an hour at a time spent interpreting will be enough; plan their changeovers at convenient points in the speeches.

If funds are really tight there may be others who will come to the aid of your party. Large suppliers may contribute in return for putting up a display, and a tourist board may help, but be careful in such cases that your product or service does not become swamped. If you are a fairly small fish in a particular business segment you could liaise with a leading supplier or manufacturer to take some of your key customers to *their* conference, making your own pitch in a separate room. Handled carefully this may give the advantage of a major launch atmosphere but with a local message too; obviously you should guard against your part of the proceedings being overwhelmed.

Use your inventiveness. Plan to leave your audience feeling that you have treated them well and efficiently, without throwing money away irresponsibly.

Finally, whatever your final budget looks like, it must, absolutely *must*, include a healthy sum for contingencies because the unexpected will happen. The contingency sum needs to be even greater if you decide to venture abroad. *Don't* assume customs and practices will be the same as at home: your organization may have less clout abroad, there will probably be a more relaxed attitude to punctuality and, in general, there will be more pitfalls to offset against the undoubted attractions.

THE INVITATION

Obviously, the number of people attending will affect your cost. And when you have decided *who* to invite, consider *how* to invite them. You may not be able to decide the final details — start times, etc.

— until the whole programme is settled, but it is appropriate to consider the invitation here because its tone will condition the audience as to what to expect from the meeting. If your sales representatives get a brusque phone call telling them to drop everything and be at a certain place at a certain time, they will anticipate either redundancy or a roasting because of a drop in market share; if you are calling them together to announce a perfectly harmless happening, why alarm them unnecessarily beforehand?

An unusual invitation, such as a cut-out cardboard plate for a breakfast meeting with the time and place printed on it, may grab attention and attract a higher percentage of the uncommitted than something more formal and stereotyped, while if you have a theme for your presentation, reflect this in the invitation, whether it is printed or just by way of a letter.

Whatever form you adopt for your invitation it must be *clear* so that there is no confusion over the day and date and start and, where appropriate, finish times. If the venue is difficult to find, include details of any landmarks.

Other points to keep in mind about invitations include:

☐ The quality of the printing and the way invitation letters are set out will say something about your business efficiency, so pay attention to detail.

☐ Give the telephone number of the venue in case delegates need to be contacted while they are with you.

☐ Decide how to handle requests to send a substitute. This is rarely likely to be a problem,

although you may not wish to be fobbed off with someone from a newspaper's advertising department if you really want their star journalist at a press conference. If partners are invited you may also increasingly need to decide how to handle requests to bring partners of the same sex. It's not for me to advise you but I suspect you may have to turn a blind eye to the keyhole.
- ☐ Give some thought to *internal* invitations otherwise people inadvertently forgotten may be very hurt.
- ☐ Many trade associations keep confidential diaries of events. Check that your proposed date doesn't clash with something already planned, which may pull key people away.
- ☐ Where an overnight stay is involved, give an outline of the timetable and details of dress, particularly if there is to be a formal function.

Certain guests may need individual invitations. If you have a celebrity or even royalty present (for the opening of your new workshop extension? Dreamer) they may initially distract other members of the audience so remember to give people time to settle down before you present your big news.

Reply-paid envelopes and tear-off acceptance slips will help to give you a feel for the likely turnout and you may need to follow up over the phone nearer the date to coax key people to attend. If numbers seem likely to be light then consider 'padding' the room with your own staff to avoid an empty feeling.

SPEAKERS AND PRESENTERS

The choice of presenters to deliver information can be critical; if you are the boss of a company and, being honest with yourself, know that you are better on the shop floor than at selling, you could simply welcome your audience before handing over to someone else to do the major pitch.

When deciding who should present, remember that knowledge of a subject is a prime essential. An actor reading a script to a technical audience may pronounce the words properly yet still give the impression that he is not totally *au fait* with their meaning. You may consider an unusual approach when selecting presenters; I've seen a chef come out of a kitchen to give a marvellous address to a food company's salesforce (mind, he had been tactful enough to use their products in preparing a meal they had just enjoyed).

Where there are to be several presentations, the organizer must ensure that they are properly coordinated to avoid duplication, and this should be done at an early stage in the planning before speakers begin preparing their words. If a presentation is to be given to a series of audiences with different interests, fine tune the words to each group.

Avoid sketches featuring company personnel, no matter how keen they are on amateur dramatics; most such productions will be acutely embarrassing. Be equally cautious with two-handed presentations; these are less dangerous than sketches, but still need great care if they are not to sound forced. Give each speaker a minute or two at a time rather than one or two sentences to say because the flow will be smoother where there are fewer change points to be fluffed. Chat show formats with celebrities interviewing company executives can produce uneasy results too, if they are so over-rehearsed that it shows, or if the celebrity has been warned off all contentious issues (which are obviously what an audience really wants to learn about).

Balance the running order between heavyweight and lighter subjects, remembering at the same time to follow a logical sequence. An after-dinner speaker who is known to be humorous would be best at the end otherwise following speakers may come as an anti-climax.

For an evening function, try to avoid an endless parade of speakers; some groups seem to vie with each other to assemble the longest list. Listening to speakers as midnight approaches is no joke and if an audience is kept sitting too long it may simply switch off or, worse, become hostile.

There are several agents who supply speakers but, although they will be honest about the quality of those they represent (they wouldn't stay in business long otherwise), it adds a further safety net if someone, such as a colleague, whose judgement you trust, has heard a speaker you plan to book — someone who knows your organization is likely to be the best in advising if a particular speaker will hit the right note. Incidentally, a famous name will not always sparkle (some television personalities fare badly) but if a speaker does go down well at your function don't immediately book him for next year — you may get the same address again. Wait a year or two so that even if it is the same speech, your guests will have forgotten most of it. Politicians may add stature to your meeting but you may simply get the party line on a loosely (very loosely) relevant subject, topped and tailed with a couple of sentences to link it to your function. You may get an even greater surprise because your political guest may wish to go public on a burning issue, choosing your function at which to do so, irrespective of the relevancy.

Outside speakers must be briefed properly about any highlights, personalities and pitfalls, such as contentious issues, you would prefer them to avoid. If hiring, say, an economist for a broad overview, diplomatically suggest that the speech is related to the interests of your particular audience; they won't be over-impressed if the address was obviously prepared for a totally different group.

Wise organizers will have a contingency plan in case a speaker fails to turn up.

It may be appropriate to ask someone if they would care to say a few words of thanks on behalf of the guests after a function. Choose such people with care. Ideally, and tactfully, it should be an elder statesman among them, but not if there is any risk that he will get up to say thank you then go on to attack your discount structure or other aspects of your trading policy. It would not be an ideal end to your presentation.

CHECKLIST 15

- [ ] Someone must be in overall charge.

- [ ] Draft an outline programme. Will it meet your objective and the audience's expectations?

- [ ] Allow plenty of time.

- [ ] Is it time for a change of routine?

- [ ] Watch the 'escalation factor'.

- [ ] If using an outside organization:
    - [ ] who will be working on your project?
    - [ ] are they people you will find it easy to work with?
    - [ ] is it a one-person set-up?
    - [ ] establish clear lines of communication.

- [ ] Appoint 'noise marshals'.

- [ ] Brief a toastmaster or MC properly.

- [ ] Consider break-out rooms to aid two-way communication.

- [ ] Give the function a positive title.

- [ ] Don't make your schedule too tight.

- [ ] The style of the event may signal as much as the words.

- [ ] Write everything down and see that all involved get a copy.

☐ Allow for contingencies when budgeting.

☐ Consider a separate cost centre.

☐ The style and warmth of your invitation starts to set the mood.

☐ Plan an invitation list with care — people left off may be offended.

☐ Invitations should give details of dress to be worn if an overnight stay is involved, plus an outline timetable.

☐ Brief outside speakers carefully. Alert them to contentious issues. Make them feel welcome.

☐ Do a mild amount of 'crisis planning' — what happens if it rains, for instance?

16
VENUES

Many regular speakers will argue that a chapter covering venues should really come at the start of the three chapters directed at organizers because of the horror stories they have to tell about extraneous noises, poor seating and so on; certainly, the choice of venue can make or break a function and a wise organizer will choose with care.

Obviously, if you are using a client's premises you may have little control over where you make your presentation, but do at least try to have a look at the meeting room beforehand to get a feel for the atmosphere, as well as an idea of seating arrangements, availability of sockets and so on.

You will have more control over events held on your own premises, but guard against overfamiliarity. Take a fresh look at them and try to see your facilities through your visitors' eyes. Are the toilets clean? Is the reception area welcoming? Brief your staff about who will be coming and why, and alert your receptionists. A sign in the reception area saying 'ABC Company welcomes today...' followed by the names of visitors adds a pleasant touch. If parking is difficult, make special arrangements for key customers. Are posters on staff noticeboards up to date? Visitors may glance at them and a Christmas poster in February won't exactly convey an impression of topicality.

Your company may possess a conference room, in which case avoid following another meeting too closely. The prior session may over-run or there may be debris lying around, plus a stale smell of tobacco which can be very off-putting.

Where several presentations are to be made around the country you could consider taking your own venue with you. Conference trains are one possibility if you have the funds, while display vehicles can be hired which, with awnings attached, make pleasant meeting places. Don't forget to make adequate arrangement for toilets and heating.

If you hire a more permanent venue, first decide what image you are trying to project. Universities, for instance, hustle fairly hard for conference business and, although the accommodation may sometimes be a bit spartan, the academic air may be just right for certain presentations. But in general, trade up, not down, when selecting a venue because those people who might be intimidated in an expensive place on their own, possibly because of fright over paying the bill, will be more at ease with their peers (and the knowledge that you are paying) and therefore more demanding.

Large cities will appeal to many delegates and are likely to be reasonably accessible by trains and/or planes. Seaside towns may offer bargain rates out of season but...have you ever been to the seaside in winter? It can be bleak. Alternatively, a country venue that has good sports facilities may prove a wise choice — you may not specifically want fit delegates but the friendship that can build up among a sales team over, say, a game of golf or squash should not be neglected in your planning. This is especially useful if delegates are gathering from far-flung places and don't meet very often.

Hotel brochures may be optimistic when describing their facilities, so as an organizer you should visit a place before booking it or at least send someone you trust to do so. Does the venue specialize in meetings, or are they just tacked on to the day-to-day running of the place? Try to see another meeting in progress or, if you know someone from another company who has used the venue, ask them how it went, and if there were any snags. All too much effort? Not if you want your meeting to go well.

Remember that long thin rooms are not ideal because of the difficulty of placing seating so that everyone can see. Large rooms that can be split up with folding walls may be useful because a meeting may go better if a room is nearly full rather than half empty; if you are not sure of your numbers you may be able to fill one section before, if necessary, opening up the next. But remember the earlier warnings about noise if you book just part of such a room — do check that a jazz festival is not scheduled for an adjacent section.

Here are a few reminders when vetting a venue:

- ☐ Is there air conditioning? This is highly desirable but can be obtrusively noisy. Can it be switched off in your room or is it linked into a total system?
- ☐ Can the room be darkened should you wish to show films or slides?
- ☐ Are any chandeliers likely to get in the way of projection and, if so, can they be removed? It may be expensive to do so — get a quote.
- ☐ When can you gain access to the room to set up your displays (and of course take them down afterwards)? If you book a room for the *day* before to move your material in, be sure that you have also booked the *evening*, otherwise you

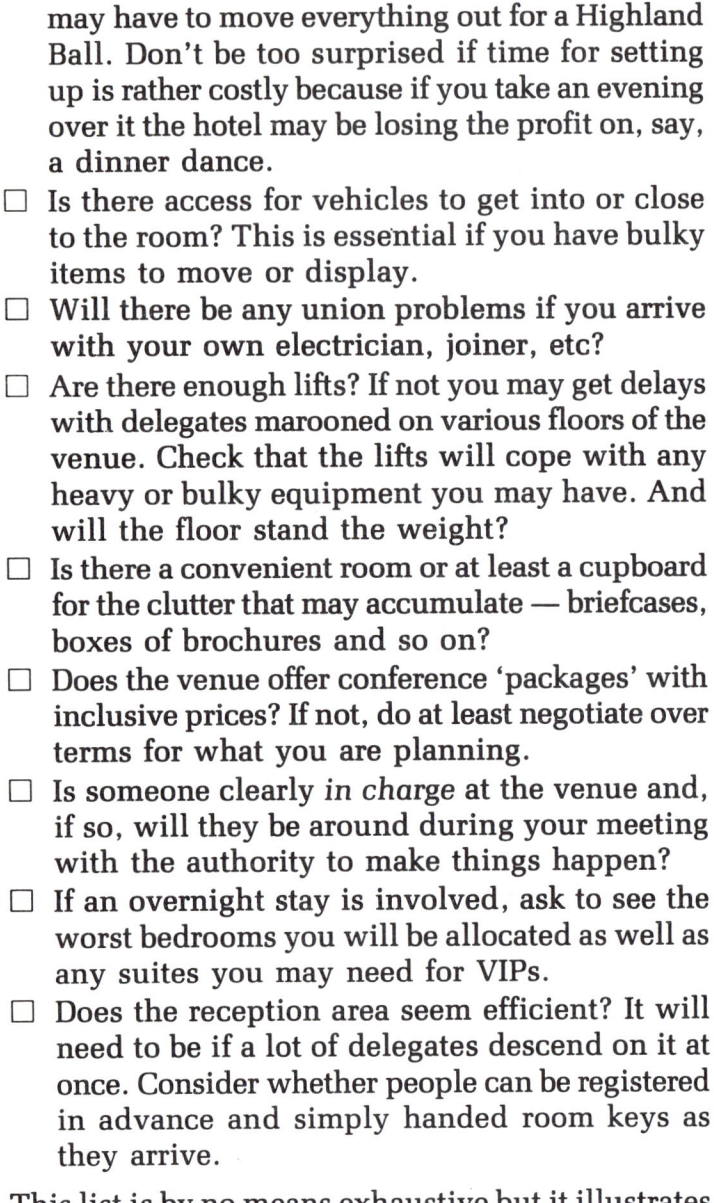

may have to move everything out for a Highland Ball. Don't be too surprised if time for setting up is rather costly because if you take an evening over it the hotel may be losing the profit on, say, a dinner dance.
- [ ] Is there access for vehicles to get into or close to the room? This is essential if you have bulky items to move or display.
- [ ] Will there be any union problems if you arrive with your own electrician, joiner, etc?
- [ ] Are there enough lifts? If not you may get delays with delegates marooned on various floors of the venue. Check that the lifts will cope with any heavy or bulky equipment you may have. And will the floor stand the weight?
- [ ] Is there a convenient room or at least a cupboard for the clutter that may accumulate — briefcases, boxes of brochures and so on?
- [ ] Does the venue offer conference 'packages' with inclusive prices? If not, do at least negotiate over terms for what you are planning.
- [ ] Is someone clearly *in charge* at the venue and, if so, will they be around during your meeting with the authority to make things happen?
- [ ] If an overnight stay is involved, ask to see the worst bedrooms you will be allocated as well as any suites you may need for VIPs.
- [ ] Does the reception area seem efficient? It will need to be if a lot of delegates descend on it at once. Consider whether people can be registered in advance and simply handed room keys as they arrive.

This list is by no means exhaustive but it illustrates how, just like speaking itself, you need to pay attention to detail to ensure success.

Once you have found the right place for your function, put the booking in writing and set out exactly what you want and when. Ask for a floor plan (or make a sketch of the layout) showing dimensions, power points and windows. Identify your contact person at the venue who should, in turn, brief the venue's staff properly. (Of the last 40 functions I have attended, all at well established hotels, the towels ran out in the cloakrooms of all but three of them. Some of them didn't even have enough coathangers in the cloakroom.)

GOING FOREIGN

There are clear advantages if you can afford to take your delegates abroad — the glamour, the excitement, the prestige. But there may also be upset stomachs, or income tax on the benefits your guests may be alleged to have received from the trip. In addition, not everyone likes flying and being cooped up in a plane can lead to stress so you should allow more time for people to unwind.

If after deliberating you still decide to take people away from it all, then give them advice on passports, visas, injections and the like, plus a leaflet on the venue as well as information on any local laws of which they may fall foul. And do prepare a more relaxed schedule than if at home — delegates will not thank you if you don't give them at least a little time to see the local sights. You will also have more time for sightseeing yourself if you use an experienced conference organizer or travel agent to handle flight tickets, customs documents for projection equipment and so on.

A few other general points on venues:

- [ ] Have proper security arrangements if expensive equipment is to be left overnight.
- [ ] Familiarize yourself with evacuation procedures in case of fire. I have an awful fear that few organizers bother to do this.
- [ ] Be absolutely clear who is doing what at a function — the table plan, the lights, etc. A small example: if the doors into a room are left open during a dinner to aid ventilation, brief someone to shut them before speeches start to keep out noise.
- [ ] Have a no-smoking section in the auditorium.
- [ ] Pay attention to traffic flow if guests are to move between a coffee area or other meeting room. Put up signs if necessary.
- [ ] Remember that a room will warm up with body heat so it should not be too hot before the audience arrives.
- [ ] Know where to get hold of a doctor. You may need one yourself if your big sales pitch falls flat.
- [ ] Put a cloth down the front of the speakers' table — the sight of ankles can be off-putting or distracting.
- [ ] Liaise closely with the venue management and ensure they are familiar with your timetable. This, for instance, will help stop liqueurs or cigars being taken round in the middle of speeches. (I don't know if you are going to believe this — I'm not sure I do — but it's true: I broke off after writing that section and switched on the TV to find a government minister in full cry before an important international group after a lunch at a top London venue. As he reached a critical point, a waiter moved in front of him to refill his wineglass then started whispering to the toastmaster standing immediately

behind him! See the importance of liaison between the venue and the organization? The waiter could, rightly, argue that he was only doing his job if no one had bothered to brief the staff).

SEATING

Unless you have only a very few words to say, your audience should be seated. Check that chairs are comfortable and are not too high or too low in relation to any tables. If people are uncomfortable they will not be able to concentrate on your words and, worse, they may become irritated. Should you find that the seats are rather numbing and there are no alternative ones available, consider building in one or two breaks to give people a chance to massage their muscles; they don't necessarily have to move outside — simply standing up and stretching where they are will refresh them.

It goes without saying, but I'd still better say it, that a venue with raked seating may be the ideal for many presentations but unfortunately this facility is not all that common. If nothing else, do at least stagger seats so that people don't sit directly behind one another. Watch for inconvenient pillars and, if possible, plan the layout so that the entrance is at the back to avoid the distraction of latecomers moving in front of speakers.

We are conditioned to look to the head of a table for the 'chief', but with a long table there may be some merit in putting the key person in the centre of one side so that they can be heard better. If possible, avoid 'opposing' sides sitting opposite one another because this may encourage any latent air of confrontation. Don't put presenters with their backs to windows; the light behind them will distract the audience and may even give them totally undeserved halos. Speakers should not be sited so they have their backs to part of the audience. Obvious, but it happens. At functions in darkened rooms, speakers should be lit enough to highlight their presence and put them 'on show', but they should not be blinded. There is no harm in 'dressing' the speaker's area a little, say with a logo or flag, although this should be kept in perspective. A dramatic company display in a village hall would look over-the-top, particularly if the remaining walls were covered with the results of a children's painting competition.

Before anyone is ushered in, check that the room is ready, with no vacuum cleaners, used coffee cups, etc. left lying around. Or half-full ashtrays. Security may be a problem if you are launching a new and highly secret product; have someone with tact on the door, or you can bet that one person who is turned away or upset will be a big customer. Your field-force should be able to recognize visitors on such occasions.

If you have theatre-style seating, reserve space at the front for speakers and then encourage the rest of the audience to move to the front — people tend to hang back.

If there is a wide centre aisle in the room, place the lectern or table to one side otherwise speakers will find themselves directly facing emptiness, which can be a shade distracting.

When planning seating for a meal, put a company staff member as host on each table. Chief organizers should have a helper in view so that they can signal if necessary during the meal and, if you are unsure of the total numbers, block off a whole table and then release it at the last moment, rather than have empty seats at every table. Some of the host company's staff could be briefed to delay sitting until they see what gaps are left to fill.

FOOD AND DRINK

Obviously, what food and drink you serve will depend on the occasion, your budget and how lavish you feel you need to be, as well as on the venue (which may be limited in what it can provide). In wishing to be hospitable, do keep in mind that an over-generous approach can actually be bad for you, not just for your digestive system but because of the impact it may have on your guests. Do you want to be seen by people as hard drinkers and lavish entertainers? If you do, then push the boat out, otherwise adopt a more modest approach, especially if you have bad news to reveal (champagne sits uneasily with an announcement of job or sales losses).

A poor meal, badly served, will not reflect well on your company so, once again, pay attention to detail. The cheapest nourishment of all may be a carafe of water on the table at a small meeting — consider adding mineral water or orange juice for variety. Almost inevitably, you will be serving coffee at some time; make it the best you can get because standards generally are pretty grim. And provide decent biscuits.

For more elaborate occasions you will need to decide whether to serve a buffet or full sit-down meal; the former may give people more chance to circulate. The practice at some university meals of guests moving round halfway through a meal to sit with a fresh group of people is a pleasant ice-breaker.

Most venues will have set packages for you to choose from, ranging from coffee and biscuits through finger buffets to full-scale banquets. Don't be too stodgy or ambitious in your choice for lunches otherwise your audience may sleep through the afternoon, and be wary of exotic menus whatever the time of day — you want to be remembered for your message not for the Turkish coffee that was left untouched. Boxed airline-type meals may sometimes be convenient but make sure that you have a convenient way of disposing of the inevitable debris and, whatever food is served, remember that the background staff, and toastmaster if you have one, will need feeding too.

If you have to move delegates around, perhaps from a meeting room to visit a warehouse, then feeding them, or at least serving coffee and drinks, on a coach will save time and may actually help to lift what might otherwise be a fairly flat part of the programme.

Take care over drinks, particularly at lunch time, or the mood may relax too much for the afternoon session to make any impact. Alcohol will change the mood during dinner too, but you are unlikely to be delivering the Gettysburg address afterwards so it is less critical. Keep a note of any clients who become morose or blatantly hostile after a few drinks; an altercation may unscramble a carefully negotiated contract.

The safest system is to serve only coffee or fruit juices before a presentation; alcohol, if appropriate, can come afterwards. I am sure you won't want to be a cheapskate, but it is worth noting that your costs will be less if people have to go to a bar to get drinks; it will take them longer than if they are able to grab them from circulating waitresses.

Guests should be quite clear who is paying; they will drink more if you are. Incidentally, if you are a wine buff, leave your knowledge at home on most business occasions; few will know or care what they are drinking, provided it is not positively unpalatable.

If you are using a venue that needs a drinks licence or an extension, then let the chosen caterers handle that side of things. Don't take chances and risk being caught breaking the law.

As many hotel rooms have mini-bars in them, you will need to decide how generous to be in filling them if an overnight stay is involved for delegates. It has been known for journalists to empty mini-bars completely when they have been on courtesy trips. It has also been known for one to drop his bag when getting on a coach and have all the bottles break...a moment to cherish.

Details, details — the key to a successful meeting. Details such as having a gavel available to call a room to order; tapping the side of a cup with a spoon will hardly make an impressive start.

CHECKLIST 16

☐ If in-house, take an outsider's look — is the place clean and welcoming?

☐ Beware following another meeting too closely into a room — it may over-run or the room smell of tobacco.

☐ The venue should reflect the image you are trying to project. As should any food and drink served — champagne does not sit easily with announcements of job losses.

☐ Visit a place before booking it if possible.

☐ Can air conditioning, phones, etc. be disconnected?

☐ Can the room be darkened if necessary for visual aids?

☐ Vet the room. Note availability of sockets, lighting, etc.

☐ Is the room big enough, strong enough if you have heavy exhibits, and with easy access for loading and unloading?

☐ Is there a nominated conference person at the venue who is clearly in charge? Does someone know how to work any equipment?

☐ Is there adequate security?

☐ Are the bedrooms adequate? Enough lifts?

- ☐ Put things in writing. Everyone involved must know who is doing what.

- ☐ Allow time for sightseeing if you run a function abroad.

- ☐ People must be able to *see*. Reserve space at the front for presenters.

- ☐ Don't turn evening functions into endurance marathons.

17
PAPERWORK

Although perhaps not as important as the venue, any printed material that is displayed or handed out can influence the impact a function has on an audience — hence this final chapter for organizers. Any printed material (including the all-important invitation) should reflect the image you are trying to project, so if you have a carefully stage-managed presentation on an amazing new communications breakthrough, don't expose delegates to 'this way' signs scribbled on scraps of cardboard.

Put all your paperwork under the control of one person who should then ensure that the company logo or conference theme appears where appropriate and that the various items have matching typefaces. Your logo should appear on visiting cards, notepaper, compliment slips, in fact all printed material, and, remember, you are never too small to need a house style.

After the basic company paperwork, the most important document for a meeting is the 'who does what and when' sheet; the 'sheet' may in fact grow into quite an encyclopaedia for bigger events. Copies should be given to everyone remotely concerned in the organization.

When more than a handful of people are attending a meeting it is worth having a signing-in book as a record, but avoid a complicated registration system; a friendly greeting is the most important thing at this point. For a fairly small number of guests, one or perhaps two visitors' books for people to sign may be adequate. Greater numbers will call for a more elaborate system, perhaps with signs indicating where particular groups — whether divided alphabetically or by, say, sales regions — should check in. The degree of effort you devote to the process will depend to some extent on whether you need to know, for follow-up action later, exactly who attended. Obviously, there will be times when you need to know the precise numbers for the caterers, but the exact count may perhaps be done most conveniently when people are seated.

If you have enough people present to make name badges desirable, make sure they can be read easily. Adhesive badges are perhaps best because they will go on ties, dresses, suits, etc. and don't reflect the light or get askew like pin-on plastic holders.

When appropriate, display an agenda for a meeting or arrange for the chairperson to outline the programme; don't keep people in the dark about what is going to happen. And don't forget to take minutes when appropriate too.

A list of attendees may be appreciated and should show companies represented too. At a meeting of about a dozen people that I attended, at which people sat down at random, the host company handed out typed seating plans within ten minutes of starting, which was a nice touch, especially as they were selling business efficiency.

If guests are staying overnight, a welcome letter should be placed in their bedrooms plus other material on the meeting where appropriate. Assume that some people will have left behind anything mailed to them in advance, so duplicate your key information and draw specific attention to any changes to the timetable.

Carry the attention to detail right down to the smallest item of paperwork. For instance, if a few seats have to be held for VIPs or presenters, then marking them with printed 'reserved' signs is neater than using odd scraps of paper, while if name cards are needed for speakers sitting at a table, perhaps to answer questions as a panel, then these too should be neatly prepared and large enough to be seen from the back of the room. A record should be kept of any questions raised; an analysis of them later may guide you in structuring future presentations.

You might like to hand out binders of information, possibly overprinted with people's names. The best way to present a complicated case may be with a one-, or at most two-, page summary, with attachments as necessary (all impeccably typed, of course). The discipline of preparing the summary should help to clarify your thinking. Allow time to prepare and collate such material then announce at the start of a meeting that there are to be handouts and that people don't need to take notes. Do have enough handouts; it looks disorganized if you have to ask people to share. Material of a confidential nature should not be left lying around a room when a meeting ends.

It may be appropriate to include your standard brochures or other literature with any material given to delegates, and this is perhaps an appropriate point to consider the quality of such material. After all, it is 'speaking' to the public about your business. If you have an excellent product but an indifferent brochure on it then you are foolishly underselling yourself, although this is perhaps less dangerous long-term than having excellent sales promotion material and an indifferent product. In either case, a customer's sense of let-down and irritation may be considerable. You don't have to (in fact, you shouldn't) rush to commission a multi-coloured coffee table publication to promote your wares, but you should have literature that is well-presented and, above all, easy to understand. It is not easy to explain technical things to the uninitiated, which is why such material should always be read by a lay person before it goes to press. Include detailed technical information by all means — but consider doing so on a page of its own with a lighter touch for the rest.

It is common practice to circulate full texts of presentations to attendees before some meetings, particularly to international ones, but is this really necessary? If you send them the words before a meeting, why bother calling them together at all? There are some benefits if people need time to ponder on, or translate, points, but the practice does not contribute to sparkling presentations or much spontaneity. You may, of course, consider having copies of your speech or presentation available to hand out to delegates and journalists; sometimes speakers summarize their words onto one page. The practice is growing of sending delegates audio or even video cassettes of speeches. Just one note of caution: don't do this with the words of guest speakers without their permission.

Giveaways? Well, however purist people may pretend to be, they tend to like small knick-knacks to take away and there is little harm, and perhaps some good, in handouts featuring your business logo. Be novel without straining too hard for originality. And don't forget children — even if customers don't use your souvenirs, it will do no harm if their kids are wearing tee-shirts with your symbol on them. But do be cautious in inflicting your company tie on people, and be *very* cautious indeed about offering souvenir gifts that are so lavish as to stray towards being bribes; many organizations (rightly) have firm policies about the acceptance of such gifts by their employees, and while many people will cheerfully grab what is going, others will be embarrassed. And guess which ones they will be — most probably the best customers. Take care.

If you have a sit-down meal you will have to decide if you need a table plan. There is a lot to be said for putting a company host on each table and then letting everyone else settle themselves, but if you want something more organized, jot your guests' names on slips of paper and shuffle them into a seating order. Put the resultant plan on prominent display. You may need place cards at tables and you may be able to combine these with menus by leaving a specific space on the front of the menus for guests' names; it saves money and time and reduces the clutter on tables.

Finally, to complete this brief interlude on organization, when you have sorted out your venue, speakers, printing, etc., take a moment to re-examine your total package, keeping in mind your original objectives. If, for instance, you have modified a section of the programme because of limitations at the venue, you may be straying from the original aims for the meeting; adjust if necessary to get back on target. In other words, be businesslike.

Checklist 17

- [ ] Printed material should reflect the image you wish to project.

- [ ] Have a consistent style.

- [ ] Prepare a detailed 'who does what and when' sheet and make sure all involved have a copy.

- [ ] Make any signing-in process painless.

- [ ] Names on lapel badges should be large.

- [ ] A list of delegates may be appreciated.

- [ ] Assume people will have left invitation letters at home — repeat key information where appropriate.

- [ ] Be wary of circulating texts in advance — information may become stale or the meeting superfluous.

- [ ] Scatter company people around the room at a dinner.

- [ ] Don't circulate recordings or videos of outside speakers without their permission.

- [ ] Don't leave confidential material lying around after a function.

- [ ] Have a final think about the overall package. Are you still meeting your objectives and your audience's expectations?

18
DEBRIEFING

Your speech or presentation is over. So you can sink to your seat, heave a sigh of relief, then drive home and forget all about it, can't you? No. To become a really efficient speaker and, not least, to help improve things next time, you should hold an inquest; perhaps 'debriefing session' sounds kinder because 'inquest' suggests that your speech or presentation perished, which I hope wasn't the case. Anyway, you should find time to reflect on all aspects of what you did and, when doing so, you should be ruthlessly self-critical. If you speak to an outside organization, your hosts will probably be very polite and enthusiastic about what you said (well, they would be, wouldn't they?) but they may just be being polite; you need a more considered view.

Make a note of how long your speech took for future guidance. Was it too long? Would they have suffered slightly more? Eventually you will be able to judge that so many of your bullet points or pages of script equal so many minutes.

Edit any notes you used before filing them so that they accurately reflect the points you made. For instance, if you left out a particular comment, perhaps because of shortage of time, then mark your notes accordingly because you may be able to use that point if you are invited to speak to the same audience again. Did you sense the audience going dead on you during one particular section? If so, find a way to strengthen it if you make a similar speech again.

If the speech went all wrong, console yourself with the thought that your audience probably won't remember a thing you said the next day anyway. I once sat through a speech by a well-known politician who got a standing ovation at the end of a brilliant conference performance. As an experiment, during a coffee break exactly 30 minutes after the speech, I asked six people if they could remember just two of the numerous points that had been made in the speech. None of them could. Unhappily, of course, this lack of attention also means that an audience won't remember many of your messages either, so don't include too many of them. Never kid yourself that you are going to move mountains, or bypasses, with one passionate speech.

Incidentally, when you get home remember to write a note of thanks if you have been put up for the night by one of the organizers. However, don't expect any thanks from outside organizations you address because most are lamentably bad at writing.

Above all, don't let your inquest turn you into a bundle of nerves about performing again because public speaking is a matter of confidence and you don't want to destroy yours; just analyse things enough to make you better next time.

For more elaborate functions (such as a special conference you may have organized) involve all the staff in the debriefing, having thanked them first, of course. This means more than asking the office junior: 'How was my presentation?' Ask staff how their contacts among the audience reacted to the presentation. Important business presentations require critical reviews like the cinema and theatre; certainly, many of the techniques are the same.

The practice is growing of sending all delegates (or a random sample of them) a questionnaire to seek their views after a meeting, and if they are asked to mark speakers for such things as style and content you may find this a useful way of learning the error of your particular ways. Such a survey doesn't need to be elaborate — if it is, few people are likely to complete it, or they will ask a junior colleage to do so — but should just be a few questions with plenty of space for delegates to add their general comments about the venue, timetable, quality of the presentations and visual aids, standard of refreshments and so on. Many people will be flattered to be asked for their views. The response rate may be greater, and more forthright, if you do not ask respondents for their names. An alternative would be to conduct a debriefing meeting with a small cross-section of the delegates.

Whether it was a business meeting with several presentations or just you talking to a small group, the key thing to establish in an inquest is whether your message really got across. Remember an earlier point: the real message is what the audience took home with them, not what you think you said. Is any further action needed? For example, if during or after a conference it was obvious that attendees were restless or angry, try to establish what particular areas caused concern and then follow them up over the next few days. If they were restless because the format was confusing or stale then you will need to re-think and re-jig before you perform again. If you were seeking to achieve certain action by your words, such as a change of attitude to customers, then try to monitor whether any improvement actually happens.

Remember to send relevant material, plus a 'sorry

you couldn't be with us' note, to absentees and, above all, follow up all promises made during a meeting (even if only to let someone know the name of your caterer).

When you've gathered all the feedback, consider whether anything else is needed to put the message across or whether the debriefing has indicated a clear need for other action. Did the meeting raise any personnel problems that need addressing? If you lost a key customer, how are you planning to win that customer back? Do you need a sales incentive to improve the performances of a flagging line? Is it time to revise your discount structure? Should you enter a monastery and take a vow of silence?

Mostly fairly obvious points, but unless you consciously conduct such a debriefing session, some of them may be neglected. And do keep a record of what happened. For business functions maintain a file with all the scripts, briefing papers, comments on the venue and so on in it. Include a marked-up copy of the timetable showing the *actual*, rather than forecast, times things happened so that you can prepare a more accurate timetable next time. For other functions at which you speak, jot on your notes any comments on the venue (such as difficulties in finding it or parking) plus any other points that will help you if you speak there again. If you end up with a pocketful of business cards, note relevant points on them to remind you who they all were plus their interests.

You may have invested quite a lot of time and money in a speech or presentation, and it is foolish not to learn from any mistakes; for instance, to be caught out by a bad venue once may be bad luck, twice will smack of incompetence on your part. Similarly, to fail to get a laugh thrice with the same joke means it is time to drop it. Although you will become more knowledgeable with experience, you should still expect to be caught out. I know I have been and audiences that I feared were 'dead' have responded well to a speech, while I have died a death in front of what appeared to be a lively bunch. I suspect the same audience eating the same meal in the same venue could respond quite differently on a different day without any logical explanation. Lode lines or pure chemistry perhaps?

But, to let my hobby-horses run wild and free just one final time: if you keep your audience in mind, find time to plan and pay attention to detail, then your road to a successful speech or presentation should become fairly smooth.

I hope this book will encourage you to speak in public more often but, without dampening your newly aroused enthusiasm, I would like to end with a mild word of caution. Making speeches or business presentations can become quite entertaining and heady, especially at the higher reaches with lavish sound and light shows. Just don't get carried away by your entry into show business but, as suggested way back in Chapter 1, be as objective as you would be, or should be, about any other aspect of your business affairs.

CHECKLIST 18

☐ Debrief so that you learn for next time.

☐ Any follow-up action needed?

☐ How long did your speech take? What modifications are needed if you give it again?

☐ Write 'thank you' letters when appropriate.

☐ Send relevant material to key absentees.

☐ Consider questionnaires to some or all of the audience to get their reactions.

☐ Note on your timetable when things actually happened.

☐ Keep a file of the function to use as a basis for next time.

☐ *Did you meet your objectives? Did your messages get across?*

☐ Finally, don't let your inquest make you neurotic — no one gets physically hurt making speeches or presentations. Persevere!

INDEX

Abbreviations, 35
Abroad, as conference venue, 183–185
Absentees, follow-up for, 201–202
Accent, 31–32, 124
Action, call for, at end of speech, 127, 201
Ad libbing, 37, 38, 70, 92, 102, 125, 129–130
Address, forms of, 45
Advertising policy, of company, 152
After-dinner speaking, 67, 91, 128, 143–145, 175
  less formal style, 62, 125
  microphones for, 118
Agenda, 139, 194
Air conditioning, in meeting room, 181
Alcohol, 101, 110, 187
  effect on audience, 12, 111, 168, 188
  licence for, 189
  and media interviews, 154
  mini-bars, 189
Annual general meeting, 37–38
  chairing of, 38
Applause, 65, 93, 129, 131, 144
Applause leaders, 65, 92–93

Arrival time, of speaker, 11–12
Auction, to raise funds, 42
Audibility, 117, 120–121
  of questions, 132–133, 141
Audience control, 84, 117, 119–120, 128
Audience participation, 4
  via questions, 25, 37, 108, 119
Audience reaction, 127–131, 199–200
Audience research, 8, 14, 35, 89, 90
Audiences, 7–8, 9–10, 19, 26, 29, 144–145
  alcohol, effect on, 12, 111, 145
  analysis of, 8, 13, 14, 35
  approach to, 8–9, 24, 28
  expectations of, 9, 13, 166
  foreign, 30–32
  how to handle, if unruly, 142, 145
  mood of, 111, 112–113, 128–129
  motivation of, 2, 90
  perception of speaker by, 19–20
Audio aid, 82–83
Authority, of speaker, 28

Back projection, 81–82

Banners, 38
Bible, quoting from, 23
Binder, use of, for notes, 57, 59, 60, 64–65
Binders of information, at functions, 195
Blackboard, 74–75
Blank slides, 78–79, 82
Books, for reference, 22–23
Boredom, 8, 69, 99, 128, 129 (see also Monotony)
Breakfast meeting, 12, 168
Bribes, 197
Brief, for speaking engagement, 14–15, 20
Briefing outside speakers, 176
Brochures, 73, 82, 195–196
Budget, for functions, 169–171
'Build-up' slides, 77–78
Bullet points, for speech notes, 61–63, 125
Business dinners, formal, 14, 22, 99
Business people, 3, 149, 157–158
  as speakers, 1, 4
Business reputation, protecting, 156
Business-speak, 35–36, 151 (see also Jargon)

Cameraderie, 1, 180
Cards, use of
  for preparing summary of speech, 23, 24, 25
  for speech notes during delivery, 63–64
Case studies, use of, 29
Chair (person), 46, 108, 132, 194
  acting as, 137–145
Change, effecting, 3, 201
Change points, for slides, 79
Character, analysing one's own, 19–20
Chat show format, 174–175
Commentary, 81
Committee, chairing of, 138–139
Communication, distorted, 4
Community relations, 80, 150–151
Company logo, 193
Computer, as visual aid, 74
Computer-generated slides, 67–68
Concentration, 113, 123
Conclusion, to speech, 27
Concordance, 23
Conference, chairing of, 140
Conference room, when to use, 179–180
Conference theme, 15, 193
Conference train, 180
Conferences, 4, 15, 91
Confidence, 61, 87, 100
Confidentiality, 70, 195
Conservationists, scrutiny by, 151
Control, of meeting, 139, 142

Controversy, 24
Courses, in public speaking, 101–102, 106
Credibility, 22, 71, 152
Crisis planning, by company, 150
Cueing systems, 59–60, 91–92
Customers, to address, 1, 9, 89, 110, 133

Debriefing, of presentation, 199–203
Delivery, of speech, 123–132, 135
Delivery rate, 58
Dinner/ball, chairing of, 143–145
Display vehicles, 180
Dress, 11, 105–106
   for TV appearances, 157–158
Dress rehearsal, 87
Drugs, effects of unpredictable, 101

Elaborate presentations, keep under control, 68–70
Electricity, 84
Embargo, on press release, 152–153
Entertaining, 2, 20, 38, 90
Environmentalists, 151, 153
Episcope, 77
Errors, in press report, 44
'Escalation factor', 68, 166

Evaluation questionnaire, 201
Examples, use of, 29
Eye contact, 70, 88, 118, 123–124, 128

Fairness, of chairperson, 137, 143
'Fall-guy', in interviews, 153
False impression, dealing with, 3
Familiarity, with one's speech, 32
'Feel' of an occasion, 3–4, 13, 39, 128
Fees, for speaking, 10–11
Fête, opening of, 41
Film, 79–80, 81
Finance, for function, 169–171
Firmness, of chairperson, 138
Flipchart, 71, 75–76
Flow, of speech, 24, 25, 27, 57
Flying, effects of, 183
Food and drink, at conferences, 187–189
Food, and speaking, 11
Foreign audience
   how to address, 30–32
   joke-telling, 55
   visual aids for, 72, 80–81
Foreign venues, 183–185
Function organizing, by outside firms, 164–165
Functions, how to organize, 163–167
   finance, 169–171

invitations, 171–173
paperwork, 193–197
programme, 167–169
speakers and presenters, 173–176
venue, 167, 179–189
Fundraising events, 42, 106–107, 109
Funeral, speaking at, 39–40

Gaffes, to avoid, 13
Gavel, 139, 142, 189
Gestures, 65, 92, 124
  cues for, 65
Good taste, 55
Grace, saying of, 45–46

Handouts, 140, 195, 196
Hecklers, 130–131
Hotels, as conference venues, 180–183
House style, 193
Humorous material
  sources of, 51
  writing of, 51–52
Humour, 12, 20, 49–50, 52–54, 107
  with foreign audience, 55
  at own expense, 126
  in visual aids, 72–73

Ideas, gathering of, 21–22
Image, of company, 180, 193
Impression, given on TV, 158
In-house training courses, 102
Indiscretion, 133, 149, 155

Inexperience, at speaking, 98–99, 100
Information, distortion of, not recommended, 21–22, 43, 71
Information flow, 4
Information gathering, 21–22
Information, grading importance of, 23
Information overload, 24
Informing, as aim, 2
Interjections, 130–131
International events, 170–171, 196
Interpreters, 31, 170–171
Interview, successful, 151–152
Interviewers, 149, 158
Interviewing techniques, 43, 149–152, 155
  for press, 152–153
  for radio, 153–157
  for TV, 153–156, 157–159
Introduction, of speakers, 108–109, 118, 126, 140–141
Invitations, to function, 171–173, 193
Involvement, of audience, 29

Jargon, 36, 151
Joke-telling, 50, 52–55, 128, 131 (see also humour)
Journalists, 43–44, 108, 150, 151–152, 152–153, 196

Key message, 25, 26–27,

126, 156
Key points, of speech, 24
Keynote speech, 15
Knowledge, of subject,
    4–5, 29, 36–37, 61,
    62–63, 89
  importance, in
      controlling nerves,
      99, 100

Lectern, 91, 117, 118, 186
  hi-tech, 65
  with light, 83
  portable, 91
Lectures, 36, 89–90
  chairing of, 140–141
  to scientific bodies, 37
Length, of speech, 31, 199
Light box, 78
Lighting, 70, 83–84, 87,
    91, 120, 181
  of speaker, 83, 84, 186
Linking passages, in
    speech, 24–25
List, of attendees, 194
Local radio, for publicity,
    157
Logo, 193
Loyal toast, 13, 46

Magazines, 152–153
Magnetic board, 75
Manner, during interview,
    151–152
Master of ceremonies,
    40–41, 46, 166
Material, how to
    assemble, 23–26
Meals, seating for,
    186–187, 197
Meaning, in speech, 2
Media, 4, 10, 151
  building good links
      with, 150–151, 159
  how to deal with, 7–8,
      43–44, 149
  interviews, 149–159
Meetings, 1, 8, 25, 142
  cost of, 1
  social value, 1
  taking the chair,
      137–138
Memorizing, not
    recommended for
    speeches, 62
Memory aids, 64–65, 93
Menu, combined with
    place card 197
Message, of speech, 3, 27,
    67, 68, 93
  timing of, 126
  as understood by
      audience, 7, 27,
      201
Microphone, 101, 107,
    117–119, 120, 132
Minutes, 194
Monotony, 90, 125 (see
    also Boredom)
Mood
  of audience, 9, 111,
      112–113, 128–129
  of speaker, 112–113
Motivation, of audience,
    2, 90
Music, use of, 68, 69, 88,
    121

Name badges, 194
Name cards, for table, 195
National anthem, 46
Natural delivery, of
    speech, 57, 60,
    124, 125

Negotiating position, signalled by speech, 3
Nervousness, 61, 97, 125
　how to control, 97–98, 99–101, 103
　reasons for, 98–99
New building, opening of, 42
Noise control, 119, 120–121, 165, 181, 184
Notes, for speech, 24–25, 27, 63, 124

Object, as visual aid, 73
Objectives
　of conference, 197
　of speech, 1–2, 93
Opening words, 25, 26
Opinion, influence on, 3
Opposition view, dealing with, 24
Organizers, of functions, 11, 12, 37, 46, 89, 109, 193
　being efficient, 10, 12, 45, 118, 121, 180–181
Organizing ability, needed by chairperson, 137, 140, 142, 144
Outside groups, addressing, 35–36
Overhead projector, 76–77

Pace, of delivery, 124–125
Pages
　limit turning over of, 58
　numbering of, 59
Panel, of speakers, 118–119, 133
　acting as chair for, 142–143
Paper, reading of, 37
Parody, of promotional song, 69
Pause points, 65
Pauses, 65, 126
　in interviews, 155
Percentages, use of, 35
Personalities, referring to, 30
Phone-in radio programme, 157
Photocopies, use of, 75, 77
Photographs, for press, 41, 153
Pie chart, 72
Place cards, 197
Podium, 91, 107, 109
Pointers, for use with visual aids, 82, 131
Political meetings, 42
　questions at, 42
Politicians, 151, 156
　as speakers, 3, 7, 42, 175–176
Presentation case, portable, 73–74
Press, 152–153 (*see also* Journalists)
Press conference, 43, 44, 153
Press release, 7, 43, 44, 153
Printed material, for functions, 193
Prizegiving, 35, 41, 121
Product launch, 2, 4
Professionalism, 68, 70, 75, 81, 82
Programme planning, for

function, 166, 167–169
Programme research (media), 153
Projection equipment, 73, 78, 79–80, 81, 82, 91, 110
  access for, 182
  taking it abroad, 183
Promotion, of company, 10–11, 35
Promptness, 11–12
Protest meeting, 38
Protocol, 45–46
Public address system, 41, 87, 107, 117, 119, 132
Public relations, 150–151, 159
Publications, understanding importance of, 152–153
Punctuality, of chairperson, 137, 139
Purpose, of speech, 1

Quantifying facts, in speech, 2
Questionnaire, for evaluation, 201
Questions, from audience, 25, 37, 59, 64, 79, 108, 119
  acting as chair for, 141–142
  how to handle, 132–135
  to a panel, 118–119, 133
  at political meetings, 42
  to raise interest, 129

Quotations, use of, 23, 51

Radio coverage, 7–8, 101, 108, 151, 153–157
Reading aloud, 93, 100
Reading, text of speech, 57–59, 60, 90, 124
Reception, at conferences, 182
Refusal, to give interview, 150
Registration, at functions, 193–194
Rehearsal
  for emergency interview, 150
  for press conference, 43
  for speech/presentation, 87–88, 90–94
Reliability, of chairperson, 137
Research, for presentation, 21
Retirement party, 38–39
Rhythm, 30
Ribaldry, 14, 41, 102
Rituals, 22
Rooms, for meetings, 181
Royalty, 45, 46, 124, 173
Running order, of speech, 23–24, 93

Sales presentation, 19, 20–21, 69, 71, 110, 195–196
School prizegiving, 35
Screen, 81
Script, 79, 106
Seaside town, as conference venue, 180
Seating, 181, 185–187
Seating plan, 197

Security arrangements, 184, 186, 195
Setting up, of meeting room, 181–182
Signposts, in speech, 126
Signs, at functions, 193, 194
Silence
  in interviews, 155
  during proceedings, 121
Sincerity, 40, 41, 42, 127
Sketches (dramatic), 174
Slang, 62
Slide presentations, 11, 67–68
Slides, 71, 77–78, 79
  blank, 78–79
  change points, 79
  computer-controlled, 88
Slogan, 27
Smoking, 46, 110, 158, 184
Song, promotional, 69
'Sound bite', 155
Sound level, checking for media interview, 154
Sources, of humorous material, 51
Souvenirs, 196–197
Speakers, multiple, 174
Speaking circuit, 10, 37
Speaking 'off the record', 152
Speaking, in series, 11–12, 13–14, 71, 121
Spectacles, 58
Speech impediment, 101
Speech writer, 32
  briefing of, 32
Speeches
  flow of, 24, 25, 27
  length of, 12
  how to plan, 20–23
Split screen, 72
'Spoken' speech, 57, 60
Spokesperson, 38, 102, 150, 159
Spontaneity, 61, 62, 125, 126, 196
  in gestures, 65, 92, 124
Spotlights, 84
Staff
  involve in debriefing, 200
  of venue, 144, 184–185
Stance, 123
Statistics, use of, 28, 71, 126
Stunts, 38
Stuttering, 101
Subject knowledge (see Knowledge of subject)
Subject matter, determining, 14–15
Support material, 82, 140, 195, 196
  to avoid misunderstanding, 4

Table plan, 197
Tact, 40
  of chairperson, 137–138
Talks, 36, 89–90
  chairing of, 140–141
Tape recorder, uses of, 57, 90
Technical information, 26
Teeth, 110–111
Text, of presentation, 196
Theme
  of conference, 15, 193
  for speech, 24
Thesaurus, use of, 22
Timetabling, 168, 169, 202

Timing
  of appeal for funds, 42
  of function, 168
  of introduction
    sequence, 88
  of jokes, 49–50, 53–54
  of speech, 91, 125–127
Title, of speech, 15
Toast, proposing, 24, 36, 99
Toastmaster, 40–41, 45, 46, 108, 166
Tone of voice, 124–125
Topical references, 52–53, 53–54
Training, for TV appearances, 158
TV coverage, 7–8, 101, 108, 151, 153–156, 157–159
TV manner, 150
Typing, of speech, 57–58

Understatement, 55
Universities, as conference venues, 180

Vehicle access, to meeting room, 182
Venue, 10, 107, 110, 167, 179–189

Video, 77, 80, 81
  for training purposes, 102
Visitors' book, 193, 194
Visual aids, 67, 70–71, 72, 93, 129, 132
  colour in, 71–2
  cost of, 70
  cueing, 60
  mechanics of, 73, 90
  as memory aid, 63
  visibility, 71
Vocabulary, 22–23, 27–28
Voice, tone of, 124–125
Vote of thanks, 40, 99

Water, for speaker, 110
Weak point, of presentation, 26
White board, 75
Wit, 50
Women, as speakers, 106, 131
Word pictures, 28–29
Word processor, use of, 58
Words, choice of, 27, 28, 29–30, 36, 93
Writing, of humorous material, 51–52